RK BOOKS

Islamic Response
to
Contemporary Challenges

Islamic Response to Contemporary Challenges

Akhtarul Wasey

SHIPRA

ISBN: 978-81-7541-397-9

First Published in India in 2008

Islamic Response to Contemporary Challenges

Published by :
SHIPRA PUBLICATIONS
115-A, Vikas Marg, Shakarpur, Delhi-110092 (India)
Tel. : 91-11-65277210, 22500954, Fax : 91-11-22458662
Email : info@shiprapublications.com
www.shiprapublications.com

To

Iram and Azhar

Kamran and Afreen

Sana and Saad

AND

Anam

.... the next generation of My Family

Acknowledgement

I owe gratitude to many friends and associates, particularly Mr. D.R. Goyal who is both a mentor and a guide to me and is like a father-figure who has supported me in my academic and social endeavours. I am also thankful to my friend since my Aligarh days and a distinguished colleague Mr. Farhat Ehsas who has always been very cooperative and supportive.

Heartfelt thanks are also due to my uncle Mr. Ahmad Ashfaq for selflessly devoting his time and energy in going through the whole book and taking care of mistakes.

I am grateful to Dr. Suhaib Alam, a young scholar at whose instance and persuasion this collection of articles is being published. I sincerely thank Mr. D. Kumar of the Shipra Publications for his personal and keen interest in bringing out this book.

I also thank Mr. Mohd. Nasim Haider, our Office Assistant who so painstakingly undertook the task of typing the manuscript.

I appreciate the interest consistently displayed by Dr. Ishtiaque Danish, Dr. Mohd. Arshad, Dr. Khalid Khan and Dr. Asim Ali Khan.

Last but not the least, I am grateful to my family particularly my wife Sabiha Wasey, for relinquishing her claim on my time and attention to enable me to dedicate myself to the pursuit of knowledge.

Prof. Akhtarul Wasey

Contents

Introduction

The articles in this compendium are written in the context of contemporary onslaught against Islam in which several countries of the world, led by today's sole superpower, the United States of America, accuse Islam of being a rigid and fanatical religion that preaches violence.

The volume is divided into four parts: the first section, is, Islam, the West and the Muslims, in which contemporary challenges have been analysed. The second section, Real Face of Islam, deals with the questions: Whether it is liberal or conservative, Islam and World Peace, Islam and Violence, Islam and Coexistence, as well as Islam and Science. The third section presents the Islamic viewpoint regarding relationship with the non-Muslim milieu. In section four I have dealt mainly with the problem of Muslim media.

The contemporary challenges are symbolized by the Huntington thesis in which a leading American scholar has sought to mobilize opinion in the non-Muslim world against the world-wide community of the followers of Islam. According to his thesis the world is faced with the inevitable prospect of Clash of Civilizations in which the Islamic Civilization will be pitted against all other civilizations of the world.

This view has been given support in the spoken, print and electronic media of the world by referring first to attacks of some US embassies in Africa and more aggressively since what has come to be known as 9/11, September 2001 attack on New York's World Trade Centre and on Pentagon in Washington.

The organisation that claimed responsibility for those attacks, Al-Qaida, has termed it as *jehad* to gain respectability in the Muslim communities of the world. Those who have been led to jump to the conclusion that these activities represent the truth or essence of Islam have not cared to understand either the mind of Al-Qaida or the fact that the mojority of Muslims in the world have not only not supported Al-Qaida but have outright condemned killing of innocent human beings. If there is no enthusiastic effusion in favour of America the reason is American polity itself; it is using the 'war against terrorism' and 'promotion of democracies' as slogans to justify its policy of economic-political domination of the world. Under the cover of those slogans it is trying to gain control over oil-rich Muslim countries of West Asia, North Africa and Central Asia. Nobody today refers to the US expert views on foreign policy; for instance, the report of a Commission on 'Strategic Energy Policy Challenges for the 21st Century' set up in the 1990s, states:

> "The United States should conduct immediate policy review toward Iraq including military, energy, economic and political diplomatic policy assessment… . The United States should then develop an integrated strategy with key allies in Europe and Asia and with key countries in the Middle East to restate goals with respect to Iraqi policy and restore a cohesive coalition of key allies."

The world has seen its gory manifestation in Iraq as also in Afghanistan. The Israeli dagger had been thrust into the heart of West Asia with the same objective and the Jewish terrorist organizations like Hagana were never given the pejorative name that is today reserved for the Muslim organizations.

However, the Muslims should not and can not rest content by pointing an accusing finger at the West. Every country formulates and pursues policies that serve its interests. If they seek to browbeat us by accusations of fanaticism, fundamentalism and as violators of human rights and dignity, they do so to establish their hegemony over the Muslim world.

Our response can not be one of counter-accusation or complaints of unfair victimisation. It is not worthy of the followers of the prophet of Islam who ushered a civilisational revolution in one of the most backward societies of the world. The message of equality, fraternity and justice that Islam gave to mankind remains the bedrock of what is today called modern polity. Under his inspiration, the Muslims of West Asia accumulated the treasures of knowledge from all corners of the world and transmitted it to Europe-the dark continent of the medieval age. It is the impulse provided by the knowledge, thus transmitted, that kicked off renaissance which has made European nations capable of scientific and technological developments as also for developing concepts of democracy and human rights.

The younger generation feels flustered and confused when they contemplate over the contemporary plight and the helplessness of the world of Islam and think of the sharp decline since the days of the Pious Caliphate (Khilafat-e-Rasheda).

It is time to introspect where the fault lies. Why is it that the lands where people were first inspired by the Prophet's message have forgotten the last message (the Khutba-al-Jum'al-wida). Why do we find those lands ruled by dictators and potentates who suppress all dissent, rob people of all democratic rights or shut their mouths with crumbs from their lavish table.

In section II, I have responded with documentary evidence to repudiate the mischievous Western accusations about the intolerant and conservative nature of Islam. The Indian experience of the British period shows how false has been the accusations and how they were based on the imperialist policy of 'Divide and Rule'.

The British historians distorted the history of the Muslim rulers and introduced the totally false view that those rulers used power to spread their religion and impose theocracy on India. That this thesis had a false bottom is proved by the evidence dug up by the Indian historians like S.R. Sharma, Harbans Mukhia, Dr. Tara Chand and Mohd. Omar.

While referring to history I have given evidence from the

writings of Maulana Azad, who advocated the universality of all religions which leads to the idea of *Wahdat-e-Deen* (oneness of faith)—the natural corollary of the faith in oneness of God. Islam forbids use of force in matters of religion and is, therefore, essentially opposed to violence.

India is the best evidence of the non-violent character of Islam and of respect for other religions by the followers of Islam. India is home to the second largest component of Muslim population of the world but there has been hardly any significant number of Indian Muslims in any terrorist organization, nor has any Indian Muslim been found engaged in terrorist activities in any part of the world.

This is because of the manner Islam got introduced to the people of this land. In South India it was brought by the Arab traders and sailors who had been visiting the coastal regions of India even before the birth of Islam in Arabia. They were some of the early converts their new religious message of human equality, fraternity and justice which deeply influenced the oppressed lower caste communities and brought to the people they met who turned to this new faith. Those Arabs were highly appreciated by the rulers of the coastal areas as they made significant contribution to the prosperity of their territory as also rendered help in conquering others. Their social appeal further enhanced this appreciation and one of the kings, Porumal, felt particularly impressed by their religion. He therefore advised his officers not to obstruct their religious activities and provide necessary facilities for constructing mosques. Of course, it was not a one-way traffic, as Maulana Sulaiman Nadvi has shown that the Hindu *bustees* in Arabia were given full facilities to set up temples and observe Hindu rites.

That Islam, at the zenith of its civilization, showed respect to Indian civilisation is evident from the conduct of Mohammad Bin Qasim who conquered Sindh and, instead of acquiring further territory, took from here scholars to Damuseas to Baghdad in order to get the Indian books on various sciences translated from Sanskrit to Arabic. These scholars were paid/ rewarded for their work and allowed to return and evidently believably no attempt was lie made to convert them to Islam.

Jawaharlal Nehru in his *Glimpses of World History* has not only shown respect for the scientific attitude of the Prophet but also argued that Muslim conquerors were not motivated by the idea of spreading Islam but by the desire to collect treasures and soldiers for use elsewhere. Indian historians subsequently have provided documentary evidence how Babar advised his son and successor Humayun to respect the religious sentiments of the Hindus and how Akbar introduced the idea of *sulh-e-kul* and started the tradition of inter-marriages and officially observing Hindu festivals like Holi and Diwali. Aurangzeb has been falsely accused of fanaticism and the oppression of non-Muslims. Although he was strict about observance of Shariat laws but that was limited to the sphere of personal life. In affairs of state he didn't deviate from justice as is shown by the letter to the governor of Benares who was given instruction to ensure that there was to be no violation of the sanctity of Hindu religion and the places of worship. He did use violent methods as in the case of his brother Dara Shikoh but that was only to acquire the throne. Otherwise why should he have taken into service Munshi Chander Bhan who had been assisting Dara Shikoh in translating Hindu scriptures.

The final and conclusive evidence is provided by the role played by Muslim *ulema* as well as common people in the freedom struggle. The first evidence of it was observed in the 1857 revolt that is rightly called as the First War of Indian Independence. It was sought to be disrupted by the colonial rulers but the later struggle under Gandhi reasserted the ideas of composite culture and common nationhood. The way Maulana Azad, the Jamiat Ulama-e-Hind and Ahrar Party opposed the Two-Nation Theory it bears testimony to that.

In the other articles included in this section have been elaborated the principles enjoined upon Muslims which inexorably lead to the conclusion that Islam is synonymous with peace, as it abhors violence and practices coexistence with non-Muslims as also its attitude to science.

The 21st century, which is in constant fear of a nuclear holocaust, can dispel the fear by following the principles enunciated in the teachings of the Qur'an and the Prophet (PBUH). The two wars in the last century led to the division of the world in two blocs, each trying to establish its hegemony over the entire globe. That led to a race for acquisition of more and more lethal weapons. What havoc the new weapons namely the nuclear weapons, can spell was seen in Hiroshima and Nagasaki, killing thousands of innocent human beings.

The power that inflicted this curse ultimately emerged as the sole superpower that is today seeking to dominate the globe. In pursuit of its goal it first declared Communism, the creed of its adversary Soviet-Union, as the enemy of freedom and when the final show-down occurred in Afghanistan, it exploited the faith of Muslims. Today it has turned round to declare Islam as the enemy of all civilizations, equated it with terrorism and declared a global war against Islam.

It has been forgotten that Islam means peace and its faith in oneness of God means it makes no difference and observes no discrimination or distinction between human beings on the basis of race or religion. Indeed it insists that differences between human beings are expression of the will of God and must be respected by ensuring justice and human rights in equal measure to Muslims and non-Muslims. In fact, according to an injunction of the Prophet a *momin*, a true and pious Muslim, is one who does good to all rising above differences of faith and ways of worship. The proof, if it be required, is there in the treaties and agreements that the Prophet concluded with his adversaries in Medina. His treatment of his persecutors who drove him and his followers from their home in Mecca amply vindicates the essentially peaceful character of the faith he preached.

What the accusers of Islam, as being terrorist and intolerant, have been doing in Iraq and Afghanistan and threaten to perpetrate in Iran has exposed the hypocrisy of their claim to fighting terrorism and promoting democracy. Saddam may not have been a model of Islamic compassion, justice and equality but the treatment meted out to him for crimes that could not be proved is neither reducing the threat of terrorism nor endearing the promoters of democracy. Similarly Taliban and Al-Qaeda were no models of the peace and justice as envisaged by Islam but their inquisitors also cannot deny that they were their own creation and were used as weapons during their confrontation with the USSR. Their conduct did little to promote world peace as was evident after the bombardment of Hiroshima and Nagasaki.

The paper on Islam and Violence carries further the argument by referring to Maulana Azad's celebrated exposition of Sura Fatiha where he describes the mental disposition of the universal man conceived by the Qur'an. "He will" the Maulana wrote, "worship the God of universal compassion and grace and will, in no sense whatever, be fettered by prejudice of race or nation or other exclusive groupings. He will be man endowed with the spirit of universal humanism."

The Qur'an has 114 chapters containing 6,666 verses. Of these 40 verses deal directly or indirectly with war. Similarly the Hadith records 83 aggressions by opponents of the Muslim community during the lifetime of the Prophet. Only on three such occasions did there occur an all out war. On the other occasions the strategy of avoiding confrontation was successfully employed. What does it show? That the Muslims may learn, by example, to use patience and avoid violence as far as possible. Violence can be the response to aggression only when driven to the wall when survival is at stake.

It concludes with the assertion, of course based on concrete evidence, that Islam seeks to raise a community of 'model human beings whose very presence extinguishes the raging fires of hatred and ill-will and who act as the champions of peace and security in the midst of a world torn apart by the animal drives of greed, selfishness, exploitation and domination. "This community has to denounce those who claim to kill human beings as human bombs in the hope to find the ultimate grace of God, are a slur on the face of humanity and of Islam."

The concepts about God and Man enunciated by Islam aren't different from the basic tenets of other religions. Its belief in the essential truth of all religions compels it to do justice to non-Muslims and observe tolerance. Thus it would lead to harmonious coexistence with non-Muslims. Its abhorrence of exclusivity frees it from the group identities of 'we' and 'they' which have led religions to bigotry and fanaticism, the sources of most social conflicts, especially in a pluralist society.

The tenets of Islam make Muslims, and for that matter any religious community, believe in ideal components of social harmony, of 'unity in diversity'. Only deviation and disregard of these principles lead to assertion or to 'separate' identities of separatism.

Islam has been distinguished by its insistence on faith being based on understanding. There is no place in its framework for blind faith. The reason why the Prophet of Islam is recognized as the 'last Prophet' *(Nabi Aakhiruzzaman)* is because he insisted on the acquisition and dissemination of knowledge as the best form of worship, the best form of showing gratitude to the creator who gave to man eyes, ears and the heart so that he could use them to explore the mysteries of nature and make use of the knowledge for promoting the welfare of mankind.

It was the self confidence generated by his approach that helped and assured the fast spread of Islam which developed into a vast empire from Atlantic in the West to the Western borders of the Indian sub-continent. This empire was not a mere territorial expansion, it had the distinction of acquiring all varieties of knowledge. It was Islam that kindled the light that led to the development of science and technology as well as democracy. Unfortunately, however, the later day Muslims neglected this heritage and became prisoners of ritualism. The words of the great Islamic scholar, Mohammad Abduh, have to be recalled to awaken the community from slumber. He had said, "Islam gave two great ideas to people which were tabooed at that time, viz., the absoluteness of free will and freedom of opinion. "It is these principles that have led to the growth of all knowledge. Sir Syed had struggled hard to inculcate this spirit in the community. The result of his efforts can be witnessed in the achievements of the great entrepreneur Azim Premji in the field of Information Technology.

We must remember that the Qur'an has repeatedly exhorted that it is incumbent on every human being to understand the world in which ha/she is living.

Section III includes articles on a variety of subjects setting forth the Islamic view on 'minority rights', 'religious pluralism', 'model of social harmony', 'social justice and gender equality', and 'national development to bridge the gap between developed and developing countries'.

On all those issues the words and deeds of the Prophet (PBUH) are based on reasoning. That to maintain peace in society it is necessary to ensure human rights for all human beings as, in the Islamic view, all human beings are creatures of God. Discrimination between them is an offence against the Almighty.

The practical forms of this idea are found in the various covenants and agreements that the Prophet made with the Christians and the Jews. The Islamic state that he set up in Madina is prototype of Islam's recognition and respect for plural society. About the protection of non-Muslims the evidence is a tradition of the Prophet which in his words are: "Beware! On the day of judgment I will stand in appeal against anyone who commits excesses against any ally (Dhimmi or Zimmi) or cuts short his rights or burdens him more than endurance and receives anything from him without his consent."

These views were later respected by the righteous Caliphs. Hazrat Umar, for example once said: "I make this will for the Caliph replacing me that he must honour the agreements reached with the people whom the Prophet of Allah (PBUH) took under his protection, defend them and ensure that they aren't burdened beyond their endurance."

While the first article of this section deals with the 'minority rights, the second places the same issue in the contemporary context wherein the development of information technology has squeezed the world necessitating a need for different societies to know, understand, and appreciate the diversities of religions and cultures. No religious or cultural community can afford any longer to remain isolated. Hence the need to develop a mindset capable of adjusting to pluralist living in a 'a globally pluralist social and cultural system'. This has led scholars to delve deep into the religio-cultural systems to discover their potential for mutual dialogue.

India, with her ethos of tolerance and coexistence, has always been a pluralist society. That is why all the religions of the world have found respectful accommodation in this country.

Islam represents the same unique character although shallow and superficial minds often accuse it of extreme intolerance and fanaticism. I have quoted the Holy Qur'an to expose this perfidy. The Qur'an says: "If thy Lord had so willed He would have made human kind one people but they will not cease to differ." (11.118)

Elsewhere it has been explained that variety, too, is willed by God so that different communities may recognise each other. The Prophet, after establishing the Islamic state, entered into agreements and covenants with non-Muslims and instructed his followers not to interfere with their rights. This injunction was also based on the following verse of the Qur'an:

> "If it had been thy Lord's wish, everyone in the world would have believed, will you then compel people, against their will, to believe."

Thus tolerance and peaceful coexistence became the ethos of Islamic polity and all the successors, Caliphs and rulers of Islam were expected to follow the same principles. Non-Muslims in the Islamic state were allowed not only to maintain the places of worship but were even helped financially to build new ones. In fact they had been vested with certain rights which were denied to Muslims. Umayyad and Abbasid rulers gave ministerial posts to non-Muslims. The health department was invariably headed by the Christians.

Islam is today pilloried on the basis of the fanatical and violent behaviour of some ignorant and misguided individuals and groups claiming to be acting in the name of Islam. Well-wishers of Muslims and Islam should clear the misunderstanding on the basis of the authentic words of the Qur'an and the practice of the Prophet. The world will then realise that Islam represents a model of communal harmony.

Essentially, a religion of peace believing in human unity and equality, Islam abhors tyranny and injustice. Justice to all, irrespective of religion, culture or sex is what Islam desires. Women, being the main source of life, can not be deprived of equal rights despite the role they play which, in few respect, is different from that of their male counterparts. The concept of gender-justice is well reflected in the following couplet of Iqbal:

> Wujoode-zan se hai tasweer-e-kainat mein rang
> Isi ke Saaz se hai zindagi ka soz-e-duroon
> (Womankind provides significance to life; from it emanates the music that expresses the innermost feelings of humankind.)

The same logic militates against the widening gap between developed and developing countries that is widening with the globalization of international economy. Islam teaches that the object of development should be all inclusive welfare within and among nations.

The Prophet placed knowledge above worship and considered the ink of the scholar superior to the blood of a martyr. It has been widely recognised that the Islamic approach to acquisition and dissemination of information about the phenomena of Nature and the evolution of history enabled Islamic civilization to acquire religion universal respect.

Educational institutions were developed for universal

dissemination of knowledge without distinction of rich and poor, of high and low. It is the knowledge spread by Islamic countries that brought enlightenment to the continent of Europe. The developed countries of the West owe a great deal to the spirit of scientific inquiry, inculcated by that knowledge. This development helped them to dominate the world. However, deprived of the moral and spiritual aspect of its teachings, they are instrumental in creating the socio-economic injustice that we see today. Even the countries claiming to be Islamic are wallowing in the same materialistic muck and have failed to provide a corrective.

If humanity has to be saved, it can be put on the right path only by individuals and groups inspired by, and knowledgeable about, the teachings of Islam. Of the three articles in Section IV, two articles on Maternal Health and Universal Health are the direct outcome of Islam's respect for human life as the will of God. The new and noteworthy is the one on Significance of Muslim Media.

The recommendation here is that Muslim media is not to be addressed exclusively to Muslim audience. When the message of Islam is meant for the entire mankind why should media, promoted by Muslims, be exclusively for Muslims. Indeed the very concept of a Muslim media is a contradiction in terms; it must be a part of mainstream media, informing and commenting on all the issues of concern to all the people. Only then will it have universal appeal and project Islamic view point on developments around.

The most glaring failure of Muslims is their inability to develop media in the language of international communication and attain the status of the lingua franca. It is confined to languages used by Muslims alone and therefore fails to develop dialogue with the non-Muslim milieu.

Another weakness is that most countries claiming to be Islamic are in practice contradiction of the Islamic principles as explained, highlighted and emphasized in the Qur'an and Hadith over and over again.

There are eight major shortcomings of our media which can be remedied if following steps are taken:

1. Train young Muslims for the profession so that they can find a place in the mainstream of media.
2. Muslim newspapers published in languages used by Muslims should reflect objectivity. That will not only earn them wider respect in the larger media fraternity but would also prove Islam's insistence on scientific inquiry and respect for Truth.
3. The community should be made aware of the character and role of media though seminars and workshops.
4. The ownership pattern of Muslim media should be changed from individual ownership to a Trust or a Limited Company.
5. Successful newspapers be asked to launch editions from different cities.

The last, but not the least important, is to develop democratic temperament in the community.

At present our media is laying stress on the Jewish-American conspiracy but that will carry conviction only if it has universal appeal and wider coverage.

I hope the readers will find this book useful for a dialogue with the non-Muslim world. I would be grateful to those who give more suggestions for meeting the challenges of today.

1

Islam, the West and Muslims

Assaults in Riyadh and Casablanca, by suicide squads, has generated an atmosphere of terror in West Asia and North Africa. It is highly injurious for the political well-being of the World of Islam as it may accelerate the growing influence of American imperialism in the Third World under the pretext of war against terrorism. After successful actions in Afghanistan and Iraq, the inebriated American policy makers may speed up efforts to change the geography of the entire region.

There is no doubt that violence of all variety, irrespective of who the perpetrator is and who the victim, deserves severest condemnation. There should be no discrimination, partiality or soft-peddling, for it weakens our claims to the peaceful and humanistic character of Islam and makes Muslims an object of ridicule in the eyes of the world.

If the present predicament of Islam, the crisis of its religious and political status and the reasons behind it are analysed, it will be found that Muslims themselves are responsible for it. Most of the Muslim majority states are still wallowing in the medieval political and social system in which the sovereignty vests in the autocratic ruler whose word is law and whose opinion reigns supreme in all matters —political economic and social. The situation is worsened by the Muslim clergy who attribute to the ruler the status of being the shadow of God on earth. People have been fragmented into tribal loyalties when antediluvian prejudices are fanned. People in these countries generally have no voice or share either in the governance or in development plans and shaping of their future.

This situation obtains at a time when the sovereignty of the people is the accepted basis of polity the world over. It is no coincidence, but a manifest reality, that the superiority that the developed countries enjoy today is mainly due to the system wherein people play a decisive role and where transparency is a norm. The most tragic aspect of all this is that these people and the community of Islam (Millat-e-Islamia) have lost lofty values of human dignity and freedom that they had the benefit of receiving in the seventh century, through the divine message spread by Prophet Mohammad, which further was exemplified by the four Righteous Caliphs of Islam.

The new generation in the Islamic world is facing a serious confusion of thought and action. They have, on one hand, developed slovenliness and inertia because of the oil wealth that has furnished them all material resources and comforts without any effort. On the other hand, the impact ideas of western education have driven them to frustration and despair about the system which they are forced to live with. With this state of mind, especially when they recall the revolution of human welfare stands in sharp contrast by their religion in the earlier era, they develop a deep hatred for their rulers' obsequious attitude towards the West. When they find that all modern ideologies are failing to meet the challenges of the times they feel there is no way except returning to the past.

Most of the rulers in the Islamic countries, who are either monarchs or autocrats, to perpetuate their power, relying more on America than on their own people. America in turn exacts the price for that support and directs their policies in its own national interests. America is condemned for acting in its own selfish interest but then it should not be overlooked that individuals, societies and states act only to serve their own interests. The real culprits are the rulers who sacrifice their people's and nation's interests for their personal or dynastic good. Fault lies not with the tiger but with those who choose to ride it in order to overawe their own people though in this process. They themselves stay frightened and dare not dismount the tiger.

For most of the last half century, the most affluent among the Muslim countries have had no well-considered foreign policy. First, they served as the cat's paw in the imperialist strategy against the then Soviet Union. Later, they were so frightened of Iran's Islamic revolution that they deployed most of their resources in 'the mother of all wars' under the leadership of Saddam Husain. After the Soviet withdrawal from Afghanistan the armed contingents, which they themselves had promoted and prepared were brought down from the position of 'mujahideen' (holy warriors) and made out to be 'terrorists' And for the misdeeds of these terrorists entire people of Afghanistan were punished. The events of Iraq need no comment; they are recent history.

Economy tells the same story. Almost all the wealth of the West Asia was deposited in American—and other European banks and the same countries were preferred for investment, too. That added to the prosperity of the developed countries whereas those who made the deposits and investments live under perpetual fear of their assets being frozen under one pretext or the other. If that capital had been utilised to build the financial and economic institutions in the region and proper investments made in the third world countries, most of the countries of Asia and Africa would have been rid of poverty and destitution and joined the ranks of the developed world. In that case most of these countries and their people would have been strong supporters of these Muslim countries and would have proved reliable allies in times of crisis.

Currently the policies adopted by the U.S.A. and its western allies are disapproved as aggressive and discriminatory by most people the world over. If the White House and Downing Street ever care to objectively look at these policies they would not find the entire world unjustified. There are many searching questions. For example, why the swiftness shown in building an alliance to punish Saddam Husain for his foolish usurpation of Kuwaiti territory, has been lacking in the case of the repeated Israel aggression aganist the Arabs Another question: if the violence of the Al-Qaida is Islamic terrorism why the violence of 'Irish Republican Army' is not termed as Christian terrorism? If this is unjustified why should Islam be held guilty for the reprehensible activities of a few misguided people, especially when it is universally known that they are the creation of America and some of its allies themselves?

Are America and its western collaborators any less responsible for the neglect of democratic, secular and modern values in the world of Islam? Haven't those who are exhorting the rest of the world for democracy not consciously adopted policies to ensure continuation of despotic rule in Muslim countries just to buttress democracy at home? Autocrats and tyrants are pawns on the chessboard of their foreign policy but the democratic elements in these countries are never cared for. It is ironical that countries like Iran and Malaysia pursue democratic policies and yet they are treated as enemies! Similarly, the American camp has never cared to appreciate the aspirations of the Palestinians who have the highest literacy rate in that region, who have been secular and democratic by nature, and where till recently religious extremism was virtually unknown. Has their just struggle even been supported and any honest effort made to restore their legitimate rights? On the contrary, a campaign of character assassination was set afoot to render Yasser Arafat ineffective among his people when he had discarded the gun and waved the olive branch. He was besieged; efforts were made to kill him and demands to exile him encouraged. Consequently extremist Palestinian groups like Hizbullah and Hamas are gaining prominence in the Palestinian struggle.

In this context the events in Algeria are also worthy of mention. When a movement was launched against military autocracy by the Islamic Salvation Front—a popularly supported religious party, the ruling junta came down heavily upon its supporters and a number of people were killed. When it was decided to ascertain the wishes of the people through electoral process, and the people expressed their preference for the Islamists, the rulers rode rough shod over the people's verdict and tightened their iron grip. What is regrettable and surprising is that the western democracies disregarded the popular verdict in favour of the military regime. It was forgotten that when the opinion of people is not honoured and the option of ballot is denied the exploited and the neglected are forced to resort to bullet. The aim of this analysis is to understand the reasons behind the present state of affairs and to identify the forces responsible for it. Helplessness and frustration cannot be the response of the people who have been fortified with the divine message *La*-Taqnatu (Despair not). Nor certainly is violence the appropriate response: it only provides strength and justification to the opponents while the Islamists lose popular support and sympathy. The key to success is the lesson given in the holy Quran, that is, to hold fast to faith, uphold right conduct, and exercise patience and perseverance. To follow the footsteps of the Prophet is the only way to establish the rule of true faith.

Today the world, which is being squeezed into a global village, can be won only through the guiding principles of peaceful coexistence enshrined in the 'Covenant of Madina'. The Prophet's last address 'Khutba Hujjat-al-Widaa', the virtual manifesto of universal brotherhood and human equality, can defeat the pernicious theory of 'Conflict of Civilizations' propounded by arrogant theorists of the West. Let us not forget that we are living not in the age of Contentious Debate but of Peaceful Dialogue. The world of Islam has to prepare itself for coming out of the rarefied atmosphere of sentimentality and stand on the solid ground of reality; they should fortify their societies by introducing respect for life, care for human rights, support to democratic values and clean conduct—tenets that constitute the essence of Islam.

Muslims have to be careful not to make more enemies if

they cannot win more friends. For instance, characterising the aggressive attitude of the American and British governments as "Crusades" would only strengthen the Bush-Blair combine. They must keep in view the support they are getting from justice-loving and humanist Christians, Jews, Hindus, Buddhists and followers of other faiths everywhere from the film city of Hollywood, the academic world of Oxford and Cambridge to the markets of New York, Paris, Tokyo and Seoul and in the political fora of Washington, London, Moscow and Madrid. Let us not forget that if Bush and Blair were the 'Crusade heroes', hundreds of Protestant priests including the Arch Bishop of Canterbury and the head of the Catholic church Pope Paul would not have openly condemned them.

The current conflict is not a Crusade but a war of neo-imperialism against humanity. Its victims have to formulate their strategy together with all those who love justice and equality, irrespective of race, religion and language. This is the age of Gandhi and Mandela not of Bush and Blair. It would, therefore, be wrong to rely solely on the ruling establishments. A more sensible strategy would be to build confidence on the basis of the civil society by establishing close and living contact at all levels.

2

The Real Face of Islam

Liberal or Conservative

THE INDIAN EXPERIENCE

India is home to the second largest segment of the Muslim population in the world, after Indonesia which also owes the gift of Islam to this land. Even if the assertion of *ulema,* about India being the first home of the first Prophet Adam (Hazrat Adam as Muslims call him) be ignored, India is among those lands where the message of Islam was the earliest to reach during the lifetime of the Prophet (PBUH). The carriers of the message were not conquerors, as was the case in Europe where Islamization was accompanied by conquests of Arab armies, and which eventually resulted in confrontation. Here the interaction was based on mutual recognition of the merits of cultures that came face to face when sea-faring Arab traders who came to India's coastal areas. They were welcomed because they significantly contributed to the prosperity of the areas concerned. The rulers of those areas provided them facilities to establish settlements and practice their religion and culture without any hindrance. Of course, it was not a one-way traffic; meritorious Indians were encouraged to go and settle on the Arabian coasts where they were allowed to build temples and call Brahmins from India to help them perform their religious rites. It was, indeed, the prototype of what is contemporarily called peaceful coexistence.

The Arab traders who visited India's coastal areas had

converted to Islam as they were influenced by the Prophet's preachings of peace, justice and human equality: attributes of Islam that characterized their trade dealings which impressed the local populations, particularly those sections that were smarting under the oppressively rigid caste system. The upper caste Namboodiri Brahmins and Nairs of Kerala, for example, treated the lower castes as untouchables who were not only not allowed to come close to them, but were careful enough to avoid even their shadows. They were forbidden to travel on roads frequented by upper caste people, nor were they allowed to enter their temples for worship. As against this the Muslims prayed together in mosques, high and low standing together. This religious equality and social justice became a natural attraction requiring no special effort for the propagation of Islam or proselytization.

Another section that had adopted Islam were the Arab sailors who brought the traders and their merchandise. Some of them settled in Kerala. They were brave people as they had to contend with their sea-faring rivals; they were also well conversant with the movement of stars and oceanography. They were seen as a valuable asset for the rulers' satisfaction of their territorial ambitions. Therefore, not only was no objection raised to their adopting the new religion but the rulers themselves felt inclined to adopt it. There is a story that Raja Cherman Perumal had invited a group of Ceylon-bound sailors to his court. He was so impressed by their views that he quietly converted to Islam and requested the sailors to take him to meet Prophet Mohammad and his companions. He could not, however, reach Medina as, during the journey he was caught by illness that proved fatal. Before breathing his last he called his attendants and advised them to go back and facilitate the propagation of Islam. The descendants of these brave sailors are called Mapillas (dear boys).

This phenomenon is markedly different from what happened in Central and West Asia, North Africa, Malaysia and Indonesia where pre-Islamic civilizations have been subsumed in Islam. Nor has the European experience been repeated where the resurgent Islam of the early period swept across that continent and was subsequently swept out. In other words, interaction of Islam with Indian civilization was more in the spirit of coexistence rather than confrontation. And from that emerged a unique concept in Islamic thought, the concept of *sulh-e-kul,* peace with all. The black-and-white division of the world into *dar-ul-Islam* and *dar-ul-harb* that had developed in an environment of hostile confrontation, had been replaced here by the benign concept of *dar-ul-amn* or *dar-ul-sulh,* the region of peace, of peaceful coexistence with those who did not accept the faith of Mohammad and followed other religions.[1]

The result of this coexistence is visible today among the Bohras and Memons of Gujarat and Maharashtra, the Moplas or Mapillas of Kerala and the Muslim population of Bengal. Its cultural manifestation is seen in the philosophy of the Vedant of Shankaracharya and Ramakrishna Paramhans as well as the Bhakti tradition of Ramanuj. Not only did the early Muslims introduce their religion and culture in these areas but made them the base for carrying the message further on to Malaysia and Indonesia that were within the trading beat of the Arabs.

As these people had encountered no hostility or resistance they and their descendants harboured no ill will or hatred against their non-Muslim neighbours, whether Hindus or Christians. Despite their orthodoxy they are considered an asset to the State as they act in unison with other religious communities.

ISLAM IN NORTH INDIA

In contrast to the coastal areas of west, south and east, the advent of Islam in north India was the result of conquests. Sindh was the first to be conquered. The conquest was easy because the ruler, Raja Dahir, was unpopular. Moreover, the expedition that was sent from Damascus was instructed to bring wealth of knowledge rather than material wealth as the

Muslim Caliphate had high regard for the attainments of these people particularly in the fields of Mathematics, Medicine and Philosophy. The leader of the expedition Mohammad bin Qasim, therefore, took with him learned scholars who translated the Sanskrit treatises into Arabic for the benefit of the population of the Muslim Empire. They were not forced to embrace Islam and were richly rewarded for their work. The Sindhi script is the legacy of that period.

Commenting on, the conquest of Sindh, D.R. Goyal writes: "It did not evoke any hostile reaction partly because the Arab rulers did not show disrespect to local beliefs and traditions. It is said that Khalifa Omar had reprimanded some of his sea-faring soldiers for their misbehaviour towards others and issued strict orders to pay due respect to other people's ideas, customs and traditions. The Hindus of Sindh were recognised and respected as believers. When Mohammad bin Qasim wrote to the Khalifa that the Hindus worshipped cow, the latter issued orders prohibiting cow-slaughter not only in Sindh but also throughout the territory under his influence. Sindh became the main channel of transmission of Hindu scientific and philosophical thought to Baghdad. Books by Brahmagupt, Charak and Susruta on medicine, pharmacology and toxicology were translated into Arabic.[2]" The liberal treatment meted out to the translators, according to Goyal, so impressed the people of Sindh that 60 per cent of Hindus voluntarily embraced Islam.

The entry of the Turks and the Mughals who came via the Khyber pass proved to be more enduring. They were primarily interested in establishing permanent and stable kingdoms rather than in the propagation of Islam. The Turks had to face the Rajput chieftains, and the threat from the Mongols who had penetrated deep into the western regions of Punjab. For them it was more important to win the affection of the local population than introducing Sharia (Islamic jurisprudence) and increasing the number of adherents to Islam.

Some writers hold the view that the Delhi Sultanate, was a theocracy and that the resources of the state were deployed for the protection and spread of Islam. There is no historical evidence to prove this contention. Historians like S.R. Sharma, on the contrary, assert that the non-Muslims enjoyed freedom of worship and 'their position was much better than that of similarly placed people in Europe whose faith differed from that of their rulers'.[3] Ziauddin Barni, on the other hand, laments that 'Muslim kings' in India were tolerant and that the Hindus were allowed to live with honour and dignity.[4] Mohammad Habib, after a thorough examination of contemporary sources, came to the conclusion that the Delhi Sultans 'paid lip service to the *sharia*'; accepted in principle to humour the *ulema,* though in practice it was not insisted.[5] Harbans Mukhia in his book *Communal-ism and the Writing of Indian History* points out that Islam 'really meant different things to different people—to Alauddin Khalji and Mohammad Tughlaq, to Akbar and Aurangzeb, to the *ulema* and Sufi saints, although they all swear by it'. When some *ulema* tried to pressurize Sultan Balban to enforce the sharia his response was, 'I am as much a Mussalman as the *ulema* but caution dictates against it.'[6]

The Mughals persisted with this policy. The founder of the Mughal Empire Babar's advice to his heir Humayun is noteworthy in this context. His bequest reads:

1. Do not allow religious fanaticism to affect your thinking. Do justice without bias. Be respectful to the rites, rituals and beliefs of the people of different faiths.
2. Avoid cow slaughter in particular. That will stand you in good stead to win over the people of Hindostan and you will bind the people of this land to yourself with the thread of gratitude.
3. Never destroy or desecrate the place of worship of any religion and always do justice so that the relationship between the ruler and the ruled may be cordial. That will ensure peace and cordiality in the land.
4. Cause of Islam will be better served by love than by oppression and force.

5. Pay due attention to different characteristics of your subjects just as you care for differences of weather in a year so that the body-politic may remain immune to disease.

The advice concludes with the exhortation: 'My son, India is the abode of people following different faiths and therefore be grateful to God Almighty who has bestowed upon you this kingdom.'

The advice remained the guiding principle of State policy throughout the Mughal period. Not only did the Mughal rulers tolerate differences of religion, they actively associated Hindus with administration, even in sensitive areas like army where they were invested with the highest ranks. Deviation, if any, was at the lower level and was not tolerated. Besides, they evinced great interest in Indian arts and encouraged their preservation and development. It took a radical form during the reign of Akbar who gave to Hindus the same rights as were enjoyed by Muslims. Even *jazia*, the tax on non-Muslims for exemption from military service, was abolished. There was no obstruction to temple construction or observance of Hindu rites and rituals. He entered into matrimonial relationship with Hindus, of course keeping in view the status of the other party. The practice continued after him so that, in the words of Mohammad Omar, 'by the time of Bahadur Shah more Indian (Hindu) blood ran in the veins of Indian Mughals and Muslims than the blood of Iran and Turan and they entirely wore local socio-cultural complexion. It was only Hindu princes who were reluctant to marry in Muslim families and, inevitably, it remained a one-way traffic.'

Hindu festivals like Holi and Diwali were celebrated in full regality and Akbar enthusiastically participated in them. There was no compulsion that Hindu wives should convert to Islam and they were free to carry on their religious practices. The result of this attitude was that common Muslims also took to celebrating Hindu festivals and even copied or adopted some of the Hindu rites and rituals—a practice still persisting in many areas, particularly in rural areas. Muslims were encouraged to study and understand Hindu scriptures and Sanskrit classics like the *Atharva Veda*, the *Mahabharat* and the *Ramayana* which were officially translated into Persian. It is noteworthy that Abdur Rahim Khan-e-Khanan, a noble of Akbar's court, was a close friend of Tulsidas and a great admirer of Lord Rama.

Akbar had issued an edict:

> In a country under one ruler it is bad that the subjects should be disunited and in conflict with one another... . We should therefore string them together in such a way that unity informs all diversity so that each community may continue to benefit from the positive values from its faith and at the same time adopt what is good in other faiths. That would be real praise and worship of God, and would bring peace to people and order in the country.

The above may well be described as the manifesto of *sulh-e-kul*.

A lot of dust has been raised by interested historians about the conduct of Aurangzeb; he is described by them as a fanatical tyrant. It is a travesty of historiography to describe the harshness of some of his acts, as inspired by his religious zeal, whereas the fact is that nothing but political considerations motivated all his public actions; of course, in his personal life he tried to live up to the standards set by the early caliphs and hardly ever used State treasury for his personal or domestic needs and strictly adhered to the Koranic commandments for a true Muslim. His treatment may have sometimes been harsh but that was only in respect of his rivals or those who strayed into a policy of religion-based discrimination. Brother Dara Shikoh was put to death not because, following his grandfather Akbar, he attempted ideological harmony between Hindus and Muslims but because his life was a constant threat to Aurangzeb's right to rule, because Dara had been nominated successor by their father Shahjahan. Had religion been the motivating force Aurangzeb would not have taken Dara's *munshi* Chander Bhan into his service and allowed him to pursue the task of discovering unity of fundamentals between Hinduism and Islam that Dara had assigned to him. Hindus continued to hold high positions in his court and army as was the practice under other Mughal sovereigns. There is overwhelming evidence to show that he gave generous grants to temples; his daughter was known to eat only after offering water in the direction of a south Indian temple.

His attitude and policies are reflected in an order sent to the governor of Benares; it reads:

> Some misguided people oppress and terrorise the people of Benares town and its suburbs and obstruct the guards and priests of its temples in performing their traditional duties. These misguided people seek to deprive these people of their rights regarding the temples. Thus these people feel greatly insecure. Hence this order in the name of His Majesty that after the receipt of this order it should be ensured that no person causes any obstruction to the Brahmins and Hindus of the area so that these people may continue to pray for eternal life for us. Implementation of this order is a must.

Tara Chand has succinctly summed up this phenomenon with the comment, 'As the storm of conquest abated and Hindus and Muslims began to live as neighbours, the long association led to efforts for understanding each others' ideas, nature, rites and rituals. Soon enough there developed harmony between the two.'

SUFI IMPACT

If Islam had found favour with a large section of population it is partly because of its humanism and equality that attracted those who were reeling under the inhuman practices of the caste hierarchy and largely on account of the Sufi approach which meant service of people and delivering the message in the language of people. As A.Q. Rafiqi points out:

> Unlike the *ulema,* the Sufis initiated a movement taking Islam from the classes to the masses. They preached equality, brotherhood, tolerance, respect for human life and devotion to God. They translated spiritual ideal of human love and goodwill into practice and identified religion with the service of humanity… . It was these spiritual masters, who were responsible for spreading Islam peacefully. Many Sufis established their *khanqahs* in far flung areas and the network of branches, which gradually emerged, helped the dissemination of Islamic spiritual values.[7]

It is noteworthy that most of these *khanqahs* were established at important Hindu centres. (The dargah of Khwaja Moinuddin Chishti, for instance, stands near the only temple of Brahma believed to be the god of creation in Rajasthan.) The population in the vicinity of the temple consisted generally of lower caste Hindus who were debarred from access to temples and also from hearing or reading the scriptures. The doors of Sufi Khanqahs were open to all and they were naturally attracted to the religion they preached. Havell says that it was the 'sociological programme' of Islam that 'won many converts for it in India'.[8]

The approach of the Sufis is well described by Khwaja Hasan Sani Nizami, the head of the dargah of Nizamuddin Chishti.

In the *khilafat nameh* issued by the renowned Sufi Saint Hazrat Sheikh Nizamuddin Aulia to Hazrat Sheikh Shamsuddin Yahya he bases his guidelines on the following Hadith or tradition of the Prophet of Islam: 'if you like I can swear by god in whose hands is my life that those humans are nearest to God who love humanity for the sake of God, and love God through mankind.'

The essence of this teaching was, that no seeker can reach the highest spiritual stage unless he keeps good company with the creatures of God. The Prophet (PBUH) also gave strict orders to Muslims to be good with their neighbours. He even said that it is not sufficient that your neighbours are not unhappy with you, but that they should be happy with you.

Khwaja Hasan Sani narrates a number of incidents showing respect and tolerance of the Sufis towards local customs, rites and rituals that continued to be observed by the local converts to Islam. For example, one of the khalifas of Moinuddin Chishti, Sufi Hamiduddin made it obligatory for people coming to see him that they should not bring non-vegetarian food with them as it could hurt the feelings of local people. It was done because the majority of people of Nagaur, where he had established his *khanqah*, were vegetarians.

Sufi influence was also facilitated by the Indian philosophy of Vedant which closely resembled Islamic monotheism or *Tawheed*. As a result, there developed an exchange or 'give-and-take' between the local saints and the Sufis leading to the growth of the Bhakti movement. The Sufis were not strict about orthodox practices of Muslim *ulema*; they did not, for instance, abhor music and *sama* was a regular part of their practice which led to innovations in Indian music such as *qawwali*. To distinguish the Sufi from the rigidly orthodox, a *mureed* (disciple) of Nizamuddin Aulia has defined a Sufi as 'a person who does not restrict himself to any one and particular influence of Islamic jurisprudence'.[9]

About the trend of intermingling of practices, Rafiqui has aptly remarked that by the time Islam came to India it had become less and less homogeneous both politically and religiously. Its wider and closer contacts with the alien religions, cultures, languages and lifestyles introduced a type of diversity in the Muslim society. In fact the emphasis on devotion to a personal God and the challenge to caste were the positive influence of Islam on Hinduism. Both the Bhakti movement and Sufism stressed what Hinduism and Islam had in common, thereby weakening the contrast in the common mind between the two faiths.

We shall see the operation of this idea when we come to consider the concept of nationalism, especially by Maulana Abul Kalam Azad, the most eminent and revered scholar of Islam and a standard bearer of united nationalism.

THE BRITISH PERIOD: DISRUPTION OF HARMONY

This process was disrupted as the British colonialists established their hegemony over the country. They were different from the earlier conquerors who made this country their permanent home and adopted policies that would contribute towards peace in the country and progress beneficial for the entire populace irrespective of religious differences. For consolidation of the empire they established social peace as a necessity; most of them resisted the religious enthusiasts or bigots' advice to accord preferential treatment to Muslims.

The British, on the contrary, felt that unity among various communities inhabiting India would be a perennial danger to their supremacy. It could not be called unfounded either because the new rulers did not identify their interests with those of the people of India. They had no sympathy either for their beliefs and cultures neither were they interested in their material welfare. This fear was intensified after the 1857 uprising in which Hindus and Muslims fought together to throw out these aliens who sought to rule by breaking their spirit and creating in them an inferiority complex with exhortations that they were not a civilized people and had never been a nation. As they had snatched the administration of the country from the Muslims, the latter were made targets of a calculated campaign of calumny and were depicted as barbarous, rapacious and fanatical religious zealots. Historians were pressed into service to depict the history of Muslim rule as a period of perpetual conflict between Hindus and Muslims; those historians exaggerated minor incidents into major conflicts ignoring the fact that the Muslim rulers' continuous attempt, as we have shown above, was not only to understand and appreciate the culture of the indigenous inhabitants and create conditions in which they could harmoniously intermingle but also integrate far-flung areas of this vast land into an empire that could lay the foundation of a composite nationhood.

Throughout the British period a policy of 'Divide and Rule'

was pursued operated, ultimately leaving this land permanently divided. Although the partition of the country was not the common man's choice, yet the Muslims who willingly opted to stay in India are being accused and blamed for it.[10] The Two-Nation Theory responsible for this division was the result of factors other than religious, British machinations being the most prominent among them.

That this is a vile canard is proved by the approach to nation formation, nationhood and struggle for national independence evinced by the most orthodox among Islamic scholars and organizations like Jamiat Ulama Hind and Ahrar Party. The idea of common, united or composite nationhood was developed and articulated by all Indians. Muslim scholars and divines made a significant contribution to the development and articulation of this concept and actively participated in the struggle against the colonial power. Hindus, on their part, shared the outrage of Muslims when European powers meted out unjust treatment to the Muslim world. The Khilafat and Non-cooperation movements generated heart-warming scenes of fellow-feeling in the form of not only suffering together but also in the appreciation of each others' sentiments.

The British countered this development by creating fears and mutural apprehensions among the major communities. It did inculcate a spirit of religion-based nationalism in a certain section of the Muslim community though it should not be forgotten that the bulk of Islamic scholars, who are considered most authentic exponents of Islam, opposed tooth and nail the concept of religion-based nationalism, not to please others but because they genuinely believed that that was the true course to be adopted in the light of the teachings of the Prophet.

In this context, I would like to draw attention towards the essence of the message of Maulana Azad, whose understanding and interpretation of the Koran is acknowledged by the world of Islam. That would be the true criterion for judging the character of Indian Islam as it reflects the attitudes of the Sufis and Muslim rulers of the medieval period. I quote the Maulana's interpretation as ably summed up by Syed Abid Husain, a former head of the Institute of Islamic Studies, Jamia Millia Islamia, New Delhi:

1. The presence of a merciful and benevolent Divinity is an argument for the need not only of prophethood but also of an after-life. Sending prophets for spiritual guidance for humankind and provision of a vaster scope than the brief earthly existence is the inevitable expression of the Divinity.
2. The inevitable consequence of this Divinity is also the concept of unity of Faith. Obviously, the path of spiritual guidance prescribed by the Divine force should be for the entire Creation and shown to all. 'Hence the Koran says that the Revelation is the universal guidance of God and has been present in the world since day one and that it is meant for all human beings... . The same universal truth it calls *"al-deen"* (the Faith), that is, the True Faith[11] for all humankind, so it appeared equally in every age and in every country. The Koran says that there is no corner of the world that is inhabited by human race and where a prophet has not appeared.[12] All prophets, whenever and wherever they appeared, showed the same path; all of them taught to be faithful to the universal law of God, that is, the law of Faith and pious conduct.'[13]

Despite this essential unity of Faith, differences in ways of worship and modes of living appeared because of the changes in time and place, so that there developed different religions. There was nothing wrong in this but when followers of these various religions deviated from their beliefs, the unity of Faith was disrupted. The Koran teaches, and demands of all communities, that the unity should be revived. It declares: 'If you return to the basic teachings of your religions which you have mutilated by deviations and accretions, my job is done, because the moment you get back to the real teaching of your religion you will be face to face with the Truth towards which I am calling you.'[14]

3. Belief in Oneness of God was a part of the essential teachings of every religion but the conceptualization through attributes led to similitude or negation of attributes that the idea of God being free from any attribute. The first concept resulted in visualizing God in human form whereas the second one refused to bind it in any form. However, the concept of this Unity presented in the Koran has arrived at a moderate point. It says, 'God has all the qualities that can be imagined by human mind but it is also unambiguously asserted that there is nothing that is similar to it.'[15]
4. Like belief in Oneness of God, piety or pious conduct is also an essential component of Faith and a pre-condition for salvation. Salvation is the reward for a life of piety. According to the Koran, God is just but He does not dispense justice as do the autocratic monarchs: reward for those who please and punishment for those who annoy. Reward and punishment are not 'conceived as action of God different from the laws and system that pervades Nature but as its constituent. According to it, the universal law is that every thing and condition has a particular effect and a specific character... . Hence, the manner in which God has imparted character and consequence to each form of matter, so has he imparted character and consequence to conduct and that is called reward and punishment.'[16]

Syed Abid Hussain rightly points out that this exegesis of the Koran was found rational and acceptable by not only the educated class of Muslims but by the community at large. This sagacious perception of the essence of religion helped Indian Muslims to adjust themselves in a milieu where they were surrounded by a large majority following a different religion. Call it catholicity or liberalism it became the basis, sometimes consciously and sometimes unconsciously, of first the State policy of Muslim rulers and later in the freedom struggle in which Muslim divines played a pioneering role in developing anti-imperialist consciousness and articulating the concept of Indian nationalism.

What is called rigidity or separatism in fact was the attitude adopted by that section only which cannot be known either for commitment or awareness of the teachings of Islam. Those who took up the flag of the Two-Nation Theory were not motivated by Islam; their motivation was more mundane as is evident from the speech of the Father of Pakistan that henceforth all inhabitants of the territory called Pakistan should think of themselves not as Hindus or Muslims but as Pakistanis.

Rather than going into the motivations of that section it is more relevant to look at the role and thought of the authentic exponents of Islam. Take Maulana Azad first who, at the nascent stage of anti-imperialist nationalism, that is essentially Indian nationalism, exhorted Indian Muslims not to be misled by the counsellors of boycotting the struggle for freedom and advised them to take a leading part in it. In his first independent political expression, Maulana Azad wrote in the weekly *Al-Hilal* (1912):

It is certain that a day will come when a political revolution will have swept India. The fetters of subjugation that she has put on her feet, will be severed by the scimitars of the 20th century winds of freedom, and all that has to be done will be done. Suppose at that time a history of India is written, do you know what it will record about seven crore people of India (the Muslim population in India at that time)?

History will record that they were a pitiable and bewitched people, who became metamorphosed into animals by magical incantations of some old high priests. They were led by the nose by their masters who made them dance to their tunes... . Alas! they were a stain of misfortune on the humanity.

It will be written that such was the pitiable condition of those people who were called Muslims, who had been chosen to receive the heritage of the world, to be the representatives of God on earth, and who were the custodians of the history of human dignity and grandeur.

The future historian who will record the chronology of events, will write that ultimately whatever had to happen happened. In the 20th century no country could remain in bondage, and none remained. The British government was a constitutional entity. It was not the autocratic rule of Chengiz Khan. Therefore it did what was expected of it, and India became independent. But the world will remember that this turn of events owed nothing to the Muslims. Muslims always preferred slavery to freedom, groveling in the dust of dignity and honour. The political independence of India is, indeed, a memorial to human dignity. But Muslims have no share in building this memorial. If amendments were made in the country's laws, if beneficial laws were introduced, if people got rid of ruinous taxation, if compulsory education was introduced, military expenses reduced and, lastly, if the country became self-governing, it was only due to the Hindus, respectable Hindus, Hindus who set an example for the Muslims by starting the political agitation and continuing it.

As for Muslims, they regarded it as a sin and remained aloof from it. And when they tried to start something, Satan exhorted them to prostrate themselves before the government, and, with tear-filled eyes beg alms from it. Beg not for a guinea or jewels, but for a rusty copper coin or a rotten crust of bread.

One can notice in this article the dismay and anger of a young man conscious of the grandeur and dignity of being a Muslim and on seeing the Muslim elite destroying it by slavish behaviour. He closes the article with this rousing call:

"You have spent many nights of stupor and intoxication. Now for God's sake stir yourselves and look how far the sun has travelled on the horizon. Where have your companions reached and how far behind are you still lingering? Do not forget what you are; Islam is making its demands on you. How long will your misdeeds pile shame on this Divine faith? How long will you allow the world to laugh at you and not shed a single tear over your dismal state? How long will the niche of Islam in India remain a gaping hole, drained of all its energy? If you must be whipped to regain sanity, are there any lashes of calamities and misfortunes which you have not received?

Remember, that for the Hindus the struggle for country's independence was a part of their patriotism. But for you it is a religious duty and should be a part of the Crusade for Allah."

The call deeply stirred the conscience of leading Islamic scholars as well as modernist leaders of the community. The head of Dąrul Uloom (Deo-band) Maulana Mahmood Hasan's reaction was, 'All of us had forgotten our real duty, *Al-Hilal* roused us to realise it.'[17] Maulana Shaukat Ali, one of the leading lights of the Khilafat Movement, said, 'Abul Kalam brought us to the path of Faith.' As a result, within a few years there evolved a unity of different religious communities and the idea of a united nationhood began to take shape. The growth of the idea was sought to be stunted and thwarted by the British imperialists who created false fears and worked on the ambitions of some to give rise to separatism which, in the background of World War I, was given the shape of demand for a separate State for the Muslims, viz., Pakistan.

Maulana Azad and all those inspired by the wave of anti-imperialist nationalism opposed it not only from the viewpoint of nationalism but also as harmful to the cause of Islam and the interests of the Muslim community. Later developments proved that Maulana's predictions were right. Not surprisingly he was called upon to head the Indian National Congress. The speech he made at its Ramgarh session (1940) is a classic enunciation of the interaction of Islamic and Hindu cultures. He declared:

> It was India's historic destiny that its soil should become the destination of races, cultures and religions. Even before the dawn of history's morning, they started their trek into

> India and the process has continued since. This vast and hospitable land welcomed them all and took them to its bosom. The last of these caravans was that of the followers of Islam, who came in the footsteps of their many predecessors and settled down here. This was the meeting point of two different currents of culture. For a time they flowed along their separate courses, but Nature's immutable law brought them together into a confluence.

This fusion was a notable historic event. Since then destiny, in her own secret ways, began to fashion a new India to take the place of old. We had brought our treasures with us to this land which was rich with its own cultural heritage. We handed over our wealth to her and she unlocked for us the doors of her own riches. We presented her with something that she needed urgently, the most precious gift in Islam's treasury, its message of democracy, human equality and brotherhood.

Further on, he said:

> These common riches are the heritage of our common nationality and we do not want to leave them and go back to the times when this adventure of a joint life had not begun. If there are any Hindus among us who want to bring back the Hindu life of a thousand years ago and more, they are just dreaming and such dreams cannot become real. Likewise, if there are any Muslims who wish to revive their past civilization and culture, which they brought a thousand years ago from Iran and Central Asia, they too dream and the sooner they wake up the better. These are unnatural fancies and they cannot take root in the soil of reality. I am one of those who believe that revivalism may be necessary in religion, but in matters of culture the same revivalism is a denial of progress.

Our shared life of a thousand years has forged a common nationality. Such moulds cannot be artificially constructed. Nature's hidden anvils shape them over the centuries. The mould has now been cast and destiny has set her seal upon it.

Whether we like it or not, we have now become an Indian nation, united and indivisible. No false idea of separatism can break our oneness. We must accept the inexorable logic of facts and apply ourselves to fashion our future destiny.

While saying this he was not forsaking his commitment to religion of Islam and its traditions. Before expounding the idea of common nationhood, he declared:

> I am a Muslim and profoundly conscious of the fact that I have inherited Islam's glorious traditions of the last thirteen hundred years. I am not prepared to lose even a small part of that legacy. The history and teachings of Islam, its arts and letters, its civilisation and culture, are a part of my assets and it is my duty to guard and cherish them. As a Muslim I have a special identity in the field of religion and culture and I cannot tolerate any undue interference with it. But, with all these feelings, I have another equally deep realisation, born out of my life's experience, which is strengthened and not hindered by the spirit of Islam. I am equally proud of the fact that I am an Indian, an essential part of the indivisible unity of Indian nationhood, a vital factor in its total make-up without which this noble edifice will remain incomplete. I can never give up this sincere claim.

It was not the dream of an idealist. That it was lofty articulation of a concrete reality is evident from the fact that most of the adherents of Islamic tradition stood by the idea of common nationhood. It was their sincerity and commitment that was a major factor in the people of India, when given a free choice through a freely elected Constituent Assembly, adopting a Constitution that enshrines the values put forth by Maulana. The common people may not be able to articulate their sentiments in the noble language of an erudite person like Maulana Azad but they are giving expression to it every day in daily commerce with people of other religions in all regions of this vast land.

Before concluding I would like to draw attention to another fact. At a time when there is a sinister tendency to equate Islam with terrorism and the allegation that Islam does not allow its adherents to live in peace with followers of other religions, it is noteworthy that hardly any reckonable number of Indian Muslims have been found associated with terrorism and no act of terrorism has found favour with any section of Indian Muslims.

NOTES

1. Author's paper 'Indo-Islamic Cultural Interface', contributed to a seminar of Indian Council of Cultural Relations, published in *Islam in India*, ed. Asghar Ali Engineer, Delhi: Shipra Publications, 2002.
2. *Ibid.*
3. S.R. Sharma, *The Religious Policy of the Mughal Emperors*, Oxford: Oxford University Press, 1940, p. 8.
4. *Fatawa-i-Jahandari*, English Translation by M. Habib and Afsar Begum, pp. 47-8.
5. *Political Theory of the Delhi Sultanate*, pp. 136-7.
6. *Communalism and the Writing of Indian History*, New Delhi, 1969, p. 25.
7. *Ibid.*, pp. 39-40.
8. E.B. Havell, *Aryan Rule in India.*
9. *Ibid.*, pp. 68-70.
10. *Ibid.*, p. 42.
11. *Tarjman-al-Qur'an*, p. 181.
12. *Ibid.*, p. 182.
13. *Ibid.*, p. 183.
14. *Ibid.*, p. 205.
15. *Ibid.*, p. 159.
16. *Ibid.*, p. 115.
17. Preface to Maulana Azad's *Tazkira* published by Maktaba Ahbab, Lahore, p. 13.

3

World Peace and Islam

All great religions of the world, including Islam, have preached, promoted and striven for peace, amity, brotherhood and co-existence contributing in their own ways to the advancement of human civilization by helping human beings to contain and curb within them the animal instincts which, if allowed a free run, may result in unimaginable dehumanisation and devastation. But it is equally true that throughout history it is the religions that have been blamed to be the cause of so much hatred and discord resulting in all sorts of conflicts and wars, though only certain fanatic followers of religion indulge in such practices. Religions are based on faith, and faith, if taken literally and outwardly, dissociated from the inner spirit and humanistic essence, very easily turns into fanaticism which is essentially the very negation of faith.

The difference and distance between faith and fanaticism has never been so ominously sharp and sickening as it is today when the entire world, including our own country, is waging a war on the worst form the religious fanaticism can take, viz., terrorism. And the irony of the situation is that the religion which is being associated and identified, though wrongly, with terrorism is Islam, a faith which stands for peace, tolerance and co-existence and does not admit any kind of coercion and persecution. This distorted projection of Islam is obviously because of the doings of certain overzealous and misguided adherents of the faith who are using this divine message of universal humanism to settle scores with certain systems which they think are against Islam or Muslims. But curiously enough in the backdrop of all the terror and destruction being perpetrated in the name of the militant *Jihad,* which actually militates against all that the term *Jihad* stands for, a new and, hence, compelling interest seems to have been generated the world over in knowing what Islam really is?

The word 'Islam' is derived from the root 'silm' which means peace and complete submission to the will of God. The word Muhammadanism as is often used for Islam is quite wrong and misleading for the Prophet of Islam never ascribed the religion to himself. To him it was a religion which he was inspired to preach, the basic idea of which is peace—peace for all mankind. The usual greeting amongst the Muslims the, 'Assalam-o-Alaikum'—peace be upon you, whoever are you, also reinforces this emphasis on peace.

Faith in the oneness of God, which is fundamental to Islam, also means faith in the oneness of mankind because the God of Islam speaks to all mankind—the children of Adam. The Qur'an says:

> "Verily We have honoured the children of Adam. We carry them on the land and the sea and have made provision of good things for them and have preferred them above many of those whom We created with a marked preferment" (17:70)

A tradition of the Prophet emphasizes the same theme:

> "The whole mankind is God's family. He holds him the dearest who does the most good to His family".

The Quran is of the view that the differences among human beings are natural and part of the divine plan. To try and steam-roll them into uniformity at any level—social, economic, political or religious—is to defy providence. The Quran says:

> "If God so willed, He could have made them a single people.

But He admits whom He will to His grace; and for the wrong-doers there will be no protector nor helper." (42:8)

The Qur'an goes much further and enjoins upon all its adherents to pay respects to all the Prophets sent by God. It says:

"The same religion has He given you as that which He enjoined on Noh, given you by revelation. And that which He revealed to Abraham and Moses and Jesus, that you may remain steadfast in religion and make no divisions..., call them (to the faith) and stand steadfast as commanded and follow not their vain desire but say: "I believe in the Book which God has sent down and I am commanded to judge justly between you. God is our lord and your lord. For us the responsibility for our deeds and for you for your deeds. There is no contention between us and you. God will bring us together, and to Him is our final goal." (42: 13-15)

When the Prophet was spreading the divine message revealed to him in Mecca he did not quarrel with those who did not believe him. Instead, he was just asked to state what precisely was the difference between him and them and that each was entitled to his way: I do not want to force you to give up your way; you should not force me to give up mine. Allah asked the Prophet to,

" Say, you that reject the faith, I worship not that which you worship, nor will you worship that which I worship. And I will not worship that which you have been wont to worship. Nor will you worship that which I worship. To you your way and to me mine." (109: 1-6)

It is the function of the prophet to make clear the difference between the right and wrong ways of life; it is for the individual to choose whether he will follow the one or the other. Whether it is a matter of one's own religion or of conversion to another, it is voluntary acceptance which makes for validity, not any kind of force. The Quran very clearly says:

" Let there be no compulsion in religion: Truth stands out clear from error: He who rejects evil and believes in God has grasped the strong branch (of grace) which can not break. Remember God hears and knows all things." (2:256)

When the Prophet has spread the message he has discharged his duty. If his words fall on deaf ears and do not produce desired results, there is no further responsibility on him to use any methods of force. For, as stated in the Quran: "We have not sent thee as an inquisitor." (17.54). Elsewhere in the Quran it has been made clear that, if an unbeliever is entirely at one's mercy, one cannot be allowed to exploit the situation in the interest of any conversion. The injunction is addressed to the Prophet himself who is the fountainhead of religion. It naturally applies even more emphatically to lesser men who followed him or may follow him and happen to have some religious or secular authority. The Prophet is asked:

"(O Prophet) if anyone from among the *mushrikin* (Polytheists) asks thee for asylum, grant it to him, so that he may hear the word of God and then escort him to where he can be secure." (9:6)

The universal man Islam has envisaged is marked by his ability to do justice to all (al-a Na, s. ie., all mankind) and not merely his co-religionists. Under no circumstances is unfairness to anyone, even the worst enemy, justified, for, according to the Quran, "all mankind is a single *ummah* or community (2.213) and the differences that divide them are there so that they may be recognized (49:13). The Quran stresses that one should do good (Ihsan, i.e., beneficence, kindness) not only to one's parents and relations but also to the orphans, the needy, the helpless, and the neighbours whether they are related to one in any way or not at all (17:24—26). This Quranic command is reinforced by a tradition of the Prophet, which says:

"A true Muslim is one who does no mischief to any other

Muslim", but "the true Momin (man of perfect faith who is superior to a formal Muslim in merit) is one who does no mischief to his neighbours" and "of whom they have no fear". Here no distinction is made between a Muslim and a non-Muslim; all his neighbours should be satisfied that there is not even a likelihood of any evil coming from him.

The Qur'an is so much concerned with justice and fair play that it enjoins the Muslims not to deal unjustly even with their proclaimed enemies. It says:

> "And let not your hatred of a folk who (once) stopped your going to the inviolable place of worship seduce you to transgress, but help ye one another unto righteousness and pious duty. Help not one another unto sin and transgression".(5:22)

Whenever the Qur'an speaks of fellow human beings (An-nas) and the importance of dealing with them justly and kindly, it does not enunciate the principle with reference to Muslims only but to all mankind, whatever their religious beliefs or social mores, with whom they may have any dealings. It insists that honesty and fairness are called for in all matters, great or small, from everyday transactions of buying and selling to national policies adopted in war and peace, whether the parties concerned are Muslims or non-Muslims. Nothing can be a greater travesty of Quranic truth than to imagine, or believe, that Muslims will not be called to account for any act of dishonesty or the breaking of faith or committing excesses against non-Muslims.

It was this attitude of compassion and forgiveness inspired by the strong sense of justice that prompted the Prophet to have mercy on those people of Mecca who had bitterly persecuted him and other Muslims. Some of his followers came to him once and requested that he invoke the wrath of God upon them. His quiet reply was: "I have not been sent to curse anyone but to be the source of Rahmat (beneficence) to all". There is yet another example of the great generosity and forgiveness that the Prophet was capable of. When he entered Mecca, his place of birth, as a victor from where he had been forced to migrate because of excessive persecution and threats of physical extermination, the Meccans were afraid that they might be punished for their misdeeds. But all that the Prophet did was that entering Mecca, seated on a camel, he was heard reciting this verse from the Qur'an:

> "There is no censure from me today on you. May God who is greatest amongst forgivers forgive you".

He also announced that the army of Muslims was not to interfere with anyone who took refuge in the Kaaba, or anyone who took refuge with a local resident, Hashim bin Khuzan, or anyone who was wounded. It was not to kill any captive, nor to follow anyone who was running away. It was truly a proclamation of general amnesty to everyone. The same practice was followed by his successors. The first Righteous Caliph Abu Bakr, while sending his army to Syria gave the following instructions to his commander-in-chief:

> "You will find amongst them persons who have devoted themselves to worship and prayer. You are not to interfere with them in any way. I direct you to observe these injunctions. Do not kill any child, woman or old man. Do not cut any fruit trees. Do not lay waste any towns or villages. Do not kill any animal except goats and camels for food. Do not burn any garden or oasis. Do not show any dishonesty in the disposal of booty. Do not show any cowardice". The fourth Righteous Caliph Ali, who was also the Prophet's son-in-law laid down these rules in greater details for the guidance of his army. The rules are:

1. Never begin a war yourself. God does not like bloodshed. Fight only in self defence.
2. Never be first to attack your enemy. Only repulse his attacks but do it bravely.
3. When reciting the Rajaz (a poetic recital before actual

fighting) do not waste your time and, instead of speaking about yourself and your deeds, speak about God and the holy Prophet.

4. Never follow and kill those who run away from the battle or an encounter. Life is dear to them; let them live as long as death permits them to do so.
5. Never kill the wounded who cannot defend themselves.
6. Never strip a dead man of his dress.
7. Never cut the nose or ears of the dead to humiliate them.
8. Never molest or outrage the modesty of a woman.
9. Never take to loot and arson.
10. Never hurt a woman even if she swears at you or hurts you.
11. Never hurt a child.
12. Never hurt an old or an enfeebled person.

It cannot be said that Islam does not envisage the possibility of use of force at all or does not stand up against those who go out of their way to deprive others of the right to follow Truth as they see it. It is certainly right to resist such encroachment of freedom but even while permitting the use of force to resist the evil, the Qur'an is always careful to point out that forgiveness is better. The Qur'an says:

> "Nor can good and evil be equal. Repel evil with good; then it will happen that he, between whom and you was enmity, will become your warm friend. And who will rise to this height (of goodness) except those who exercise patience and self-restraint and who have been given an ample share of goodness. (41:34,35)

The Qur'an calls upon all men to "cultivate in themselves the attributes of Allah". This implies that the compassion which God shows to His creatures must be mirrored in the personality of a Momin (true believer). It is a reflection of God in man. Not only in the Qur'an but also in the traditions of the Prophet, it is stressed again and again that, "If you love Allah, you must love all his creatures". This intimate relationship between love for God and love for one's fellow beings has been beautifully brought out in the form of a parable in a well-known Hadith of the Prophet:

> "On the day of judgment God will ask a man: O son of Adam, I had fallen ill and you never attended me. Surprised, he will ask: How could that be possible? Thou art the Lord of the Universe. God will reply: Do you not remember that a neighbour of yours was ill and you never turned to him in solicitude? If you had gone to see him you would have found Me by his side. Then He will ask, O son of Adam, I asked you to give Me food but you refused! The man would reply: How could Thou be in need of anything? God will reply: Do you not remember that one of My servants asked you for it but you refused. If you had fed him, you would have found Me by his side. Then He will say: I asked you for water but you did not give it to Me. Again he will ask: How is it possible that Thou, the sustainer of the worlds, should be thirsty? God will again answer: A servant of Mine asked you for water but you did not give it to him. If you had done so, you would have found Me by his side".

The essential insistence on co-existence and justice found expression in the nature and composition of the Islamic society that the Prophet established in his life time. This society presents a model for the possibility of followers of different faiths living together with honour and enjoying all human rights.

The provision of human rights to non-Muslims or minorities under the Islamic system is based on the principles of justice, oneness of man and religious tolerance. It is said that any society is democratic only to the extent and measure it protects the rights of its minorities. Islam not only applied this yardstick but also institutionalised it to the extent that the Prophet of Islam while showing concern for the protection of the rights of non-Muslims exhorted: "Beware! On the day of Judgment I will stand in appeal against anyone who commits excesses against any ally (*dhimmi*) or cuts short his rights or burdens him more than endurance or receives anything from him without his consent (Abu Dawood, Kitab-al-Jihad).

The Prophet concluded many treaties and Tribute Agreements with different people. The agreement concluded between the Prophet and the Christians of Sinai went as follows:

> "...This is a writ according to which a treaty is concluded with them and whoever oppose its articles will be considered a transgressor to him (the Prophet) and other Muslims. Such a person will be rejecting Allah's promise...

...Whenever monks or travellers get together, and reside in the mountains or in the desert, in inhabited places or in plane, in synagogues or temples, we will be behind them to preserve and protect them, and I will defend their lives, property and goods with my life and that of my friends, helpers and nation, since they are my subjects and united allies.

With the exception of what they willingly pay as tribute, they will by no means be compelled to pay anything more or held responsible for it.

Their judges, monks, hermits and travellers will not be molested and no synagogue or church will be destroyed and nothing of their property may enter the Muslims' dwellings" (Ibn Hisham's Sirah. Vol. 2)

The Righteous Caliphs, too, strictly followed the principles set by the Prophet (PBUH). During the time of the first Pious Caliph Abu Bakr a non-Muslim woman who abused Muslims had her teeth broken by some Muslims. On coming to know of the matter the Caliph wrote to his officer Mahajir Bin Umayyah:

> "I have come to know that you have got two of the upper teeth of the woman who sang derogatory verses against Muslims broken. A warning could have been sufficient had she been a Muslim and her punishment must be less than a reprimand. Being a *dhimmi* her singing these verses is nothing, when her sin is as great as Shirk, is being tolerated. Had I been able to warn you earlier you must have tasted the punishment for your excess."

The second Righteous Caliph Umar was so concerned about the treatment to the *dhimmis* that even on his death bed he made the will:

> "I make this will for the Caliph replacing me that he must honour the agreement reached with the people whom the Prophet of Allah (PBUH) took under his protection, defend them and ensure that they are not burdened beyond their endurance".

The Islamic state is bound to honour, implement and protect the rights of the non-Muslims and no Muslim has a right to tamper with or alter them as these are the rights established and ordained by the Qur'an and the Sunnah. Muslims and non-Muslims are at par in an Islamic state from the standpoint of protection of rights. In a way non-Muslims enjoy an edge over the Muslims in this regard as the Islamic state may impose additional taxes on the Muslims or acquire their property under special circumstances but it cannot overburden the *dhimmis* after the agreement with them is finalised.

In the Islamic state the civil and penal laws of Islam are equally applicable to the non-Muslims except with regard to the consumption of alcohol. According to Imam Malik they enjoy exemption even with regard to fornication. Non-Muslims are free to brew, drink and sell wine among themselves and to keep, eat and sell wines among themselves. The Islamic State allows personal matters of non-Muslims to be judged by their Personal Laws. Khwaja Hasan Basri decreed on a query from the Caliph Umar Bin Abd-al-Aziz:

> "They have consented to pay *Jazya* on the condition that they will be granted freedom to lead their lives according to their faith. You must follow the established path and not invent any new way."

Non-Muslims are also free to arrange for the education of

their children the way they like, establish educational institutions and propagate their religion among themselves.

There is of course much more that a penetrative and exhaustive study of Islam can reveal but the outline of the fundamental principles enshrined in the Qur'an and the traditions of the Prophet I have tried to sketch brings out clearly that the twin Islamic principles of tolerance and justice have been the motive force behind the making of an Islamic individual and society. These two principles are a gift of Islam to human civilization, a call to human beings to live in peace and harmony, rising above all the differences of faith, colour or race. It is a call to Muslims and non-Muslim alike. Whoever responds to this call will be an ally in the task of human reconstruction and civilizational regeneration in the 21st century.

The Qur'an depicts God as almighty but it also depicts Him as beneficent and merciful. God's creation is a gift of God's grace. A Hadith says: When God completed the creation He wrote the following which is with Him above His throne, "My mercy has taken precedence over my anger".

In Islamic tradition both the sovereignty and beneficence of Allah are described as present realities, indicating that the creative power of God continues to be expressed in Allah's on-going creation of the world. Allah is sustainer and guide of all life, in the present as well as the past. There is a sense in which it may be said that Allah continually recreates the world every moment or as the Qur'an puts it, "God originates creation, then repeats it." This aspect of Allah's creativity is given special emphasis when human birth is discussed; the fetal development of humans is attributed to the creative power of Allah. The creation theology of Islam then, is not intended primarily to describe some primordial act of God's creativity but rather confess Allah's ongoing creative role in the present life of believers and their world.

Allah, the Qur'an says, created the world neither "in jest" nor "for naught", that is, God has a serious purpose for the creation. The purpose of creation is to serve Allah and to submit to His will. This view of creation implies that the creation of primary function is religious or devotional which means that Allah's creation is good and appropriately prompts a response of praise. Human beings are expected to respond to the honour Allah bestowes on them with worship and gratitude. The status of vice-regency bestowed on Man is a test to see if he obeys the will of Allah and acknowledges His sovereignty in an attitude of humility, repentance, loyalty and faith. Another purpose of creation is to provide signs of Allah's sovereignty and beneficence. These signs are intended less to provide an intellectual proof for the creative activity of God than to evoke gratitude in humans as they observe the wonders of creation.

Noteworthy is also the fact that this devotional purpose applies to the non-human creation too. "Whatever is in heavens and in earth—let it declare the praises and glory of God: for He is the exalted in might, wise". (57:1). "From the thunder to the angels, from the birds to the hills, all creation is to join in the praise of Allah" (13:14). It suggests that all of creation should be respected by humans as it also worships Allah. Islam values all life, not just human life. Animals are to be treated with compassion and concern, partly because they are God's creation, partly because they have a role to play in the devotional functions of all creation.

The Qur'an considers non-human living beings as communities. It says: "There is no animal on earth, nor a bird that flies with its two wings, but they are communities like your own" (6.38)

One may tend to believe that the status of vice-gerency bestowed on man in Islam entails that man has been given the authority to control all the creation and the environment to his will. But the Islamic emphasis on the sovereignty of God out-weighs such consequences of the human vice-gerency which in essence means exercising care for the rest of the creation, not violating or exploiting it wantonly.

Life in the Islamic world view is a trust that God has bestowed on man. It is a gift of God to man. It must be preserved and cultivated and lived in the service of God and fellow human beings, and not be wasted in vain. That is also why Islam forbids suicide as man does not own his life but is just a trustee of it.

Like life, the physical health is also a gift of God which should be protected from illness. There are many sayings of the prophet which stress the importance of health and treatment of illness.

A tradition says: "Healthiness and freedom (from stress, strain and hardship) are two of the most precious gifts of God. (Zad-at Ma'ad).

The Prophet has exhorted his followers to seek treatment of illness. He says: "God has not created any illness for which He has not created a medicine (Bukhari, Muslim) According to another tradition: "Some Bedouins once asked the Prophet "O Messenger of God: If we do not seek treatment will it be a sin for us? The Prophet replied "Yes, O, slaves of God! You must seek treatment for yourselves. God has not created an ailment but for one that does not have remedy." They enquired "what is that ailment". The Prophet replied, "That is senility". (Tirmidhi, Nasai, Ibn Majah).

These categorical declarations that there is a remedy for every ailment and that to seek treatment is not a sin proved to be very revolutionary at a time when diseases were considered all over the world to be signs of divine displeasure and the only remedy in popular perception was offering sacrifices to gods. This also proved to be a source of hope for patients. Moreover, it encouraged and inspired a process of research in medical science which the Muslim scientists raised to great heights.

Lastly a word on the Prophet's attitude towards leprosy and its victims. In an age when leprosy was taken as a sign of divine wrath and a scourge, and the lepers were abandoned and secluded to fend for themselves, the Prophet of Islam, according to a Hadith, held the hand of a leprosy patient and made him to eat from his bowl, saying: "Eat in the name of Allah and have trust in Him" (Tirmidhi). This is only natural for a Prophet who, according to the Qur'an, has been sent as a mercy on all mankind. By this uncommon act of kindness he removed the horror and stigma attached to a leprosy patient, recognising him as a human being afflicted by a disease which can be cured.

4

Islam and Violence

Islam and violence are mutually contradictory. The word 'Islam', from its root s-l-m literally means peace and submission. A Muslim greets others with the words *Assalam-o-Alaikum* which means 'peace be on you' and the return greeting *wa-alaikum-as-salam* also denotes the same: 'peace be on you, too.' A Muslim starts his work with the invocation *Bismillah al-Rahman-al-Rahim,* meaning 'In the name of Allah, the Compassionate, the Merciful.' The first Surah (Chapter) of the Qur'an, *Surah Al-Fatiha,* the Opening, which is considered an *epitome* of the entire Islamic teachings and which a Muslim recites in all the prayers, begins with the words: 'Praise be to Allah, the Beneficent, the Merciful.' The Prophet of Islam (PBUH) has been described in the Qur'an as sent by God to be a source of mercy and kindness to all mankind. Such repeated insistence on peace, mercy and beneficence underlines the essential defining character of Islamic message as well as the kind of human attitude and behaviour Islam essentialises for the believers.

Islam primarily emphasizes two of the cardinal principles, faith in God and good deeds, to guide the shaping of the individual human being in a way that one develops into a positive, creative, constructive and responsible member of a human society which is bound to reflect the values of fraternity, equality, justice and co-existence if it is formed of the individuals having the same attributes. For Islam this world of good and evil and sweat and blood of human actions is as important as the world to come, the

Hereafter. Islam has demolished the dualism postulated between the worlds of Here and Hereafter, between matter and spirit. It enjoins upon all believers to pray, 'Lord! Give me the good things of this world and the good things of the Hereafter.' This is not greed and *avarice*, asking for material comforts but a realization of the profound truth that these good things are inter-related and parts of a material-spiritual continuum. The Prophet (PBUH) in one of his sayings reinforces this truth by remarking that 'this world is the field that one ploughs for the world to come.' This is only to emphasize that whatever man does here in this world is being watched by the Omnipresent and Omniscient God and will be rewarded on the Day of Judgment according to the merits of human actions. Thus for a man who needs the divine message, the very act of living becomes an act of worship.

To create, promote and sustain an individual and a society which is peace-loving, just, and believes in co-existence, Islam has laid down a set of principles that help produce the environment and ambience—intellectual, moral, social and spiritual—conducive to the emergence of such an individual and social setting. One such principle is the Islamic concept of all men and women being members of one single human family, who are bound together by inalienable bonds of brotherhood, having goodwill towards each other and helping each other in making this world worthy of civilized human existence. The Qur'an says: 'Men, have fear of your Lord, who created you from a single soul. From that soul He created its mate, and through them He bestrewed the earth with countless men and women.' (4:1). Here the Qur'an addresses not specifically Muslims but all human beings in general and refers to their common origin and descent. The Prophet (PBUH) reinforces this theme by saying: 'you all have been created through Adam and Adam was brought forth from clay.' In his last and departing Haj sermon, which stands as the charter of universal humanism enunciated about 1400 years back, the Prophet (PBUH) emphatically stresses: "No Arab has any superiority over a non-Arab, nor any Ajam (Iranian) enjoys any exaltedness over any Arab; neither a black is superior to a white nor a white is exalted over a black, except the one who earns superiority through fear of God." What the Qur'an and the Prophet (PBUH) intend here is to create the ideal of the universal man out of the narrow, selfish, greed-struck, earth-rooted and material-bound man as we find him. Maulana Azad in his highly celebrated commentary on the Surah Al-Fatiha of the Qur'an characterizes this universal man in the following words:

> Such a person passionately chants the glory and praise of God, not a God claimed as their own by different races and nations and creeds but the Beneficent, Creator of the entire universe, whose mercy and compassion encompass the whole human race. When he wishes to invoke His attributes, only two come to his mind irresistibly—His compassion and His justice—which comprise for him the essence of His being. Then he bows his head in obeisance to Him in implicit, undivided allegiance. "Before Thee alone, O Lord, do I bow my head and from Thee alone do I seek help in all my needs and tribulations". Thus focussing his devotion and his prayer for help and guidance on Him alone, he becomes indifferent to, and fearless of, all citadels of power and prestige built by man. He will not bow his head now at any other threshold, nor be afraid of any other power, nor extend a beggar's hand at any other door. Then, he prays for God's grace to follow the right path—the only favour that his tongue is prepared to ask. And what is this right, this straight path? Is it the path of some particular nation or race? Of some particular religious group? No, it is the common path which all the great religious leaders of mankind, all the truth-loving, truth-seeking men and women of the world have trodden, whatever the age or race to which they belonged. Likewise, he prays to be shielded from the path of transgression and wrong. But here, too, there is no reference to any particular race or creed or nation but to the way of all those who have fallen from grace and been led astray. Thus what he passionately desires is the universal good of all mankind and what he passionately rejects is that which is

evil for all mankind. Differences of race, nation, community or creed—discrimination of any kind based on such considerations—do not cast their faintest shadow on his heart and mind. What then is the kind of mould in which the mind of such a person will be cast? He will worship the God of universal compassion and grace and will, in no sense, whatever, be fettered by prejudices of race or nation or other exclusive groupings. He will be man endowed with the spirit of universal humanism!

The second principle that Islam stresses is that human life is sacrosanct. Under Islamic dispensation sanctity and security of life, property and honour of all human beings, Muslim or non-Muslim, is assured. Killing a human being without any reason is just unacceptable to Islam. The Qur'an ordains: 'Whoever killed a human being, except as a punishment for murder or sedition in earth, should be looked upon as though he had killed all mankind; and whoever saved a human life should be regarded as though he had saved all mankind' (5:32). Islam denounces all forms of *wanton* violence, aggression, destruction and mischief and calls them as the acts of the Satan. The Qur'an reprimands: 'Do not make mischief on the earth after it has been purged' (7:56). It again warns: 'Fight for the sake of Allah those who fight against you, but do not commit aggression. Allah does not like the aggressors.' (2.190). In Islam, use of violence is permitted only in self-defence and to ward off evil. Violence *per se* has no place in Islam. The Qur'an is very explicit in this regard as it says: 'permission to fight is given to those who are attacked.' (22:39). Islam does not consider violence to be a permanent situation in human affairs. It is always an exception rather than a rule, according to the Quranic perception. The Qur'an impresses upon human beings that an enemy today can turn into a friend in future and as such all enemies can be taken as potential friends if they are viewed in the light of the large-heartedness and compassion that Islam intends to develop in human beings. These Quranic verses are clear guidance in this regard: 'And good and evil are not alike. Requite evil with what is best. Then truly he, between whom and you there was enmity, will become your dearest friend." (41:34).

In the face of aggression and violence the best response according to Islam is patience and worship. Islam stresses to avoid to the unmost limits of endurance the use of counter-violence. Before that, according to the Qur'an, "Reconciliation is best" (4:128). It is the basic spirit of Islam that when conflict is unavoidable and hostilities are on, even in that situation reconciliation should have to be resorted to in order to bring the hostilities to an end. It is because conflict is always an unnatural situation and is detested by the inner most core of humanness which is rooted in peace and co-existence. The Prophet (PBUH) recommends to the believers: 'You should not desire confrontation with the enemy; you should ask God for peace.' The Quranic verse reinforces the same spirit by saying: 'Whenever they kindle the fire of war, Allah puts it out.'

The Qur'an has 114 chapters in all containing 6,666 verses and only 40 verses deal directly or indirectly with war. In the same way when the Prophet (PBUH) was faced with aggression from his opponents and according to the Hadith records 83 such aggressions against the Islamic community were attempted by the opponents but due to the strategy of avoidance of confrontation employed by the Prophet (PBUH) only three all-out battles, Badr, Uhud and Hunain, could take place. The highest example of avoidance of confrontation and violence and spirit of reconciliation set by the Prophet (PBUH) was the famous Hudaibia peace treaty that the Prophet concluded with his opponents when war seemed imminent between the believers and their opponents. The Prophet, to the astonishment of all-in his or the enemy camp-initiated peace negotiations in which the opponents proved to be hard bargainers and put strong conditions that under no circumstances could be accepted, no matter how much peace-loving one could be. But the Prophet unilaterally accepted all the conditions, some seemingly quite humiliating, and restored peace.

The treaty provided the *nascent* Islamic community the much needed breathing space and the Muslims utilized the opportunity to spread the message of Islam far and wide. As a result, the whole of Arabian peninsula came under the Islamic umbrella within no time.

According to Islamic teachings, only the established governments can wage war and that, too, with proper declaration. No individuals or non-government organizations have any right or religio-legal sanction to initiate combat operations against any real or perceived enemy or threat. The above-quoted verse, "And fight in the way of Allah with those who fight you, but do not be aggressive. Allah does not like aggressors", is very explicit that permission to wage war is granted in Islam only in case a party has already initiated hostilities against the Islamic community, unilaterally. This means that in Islam war is always defensive. The basic principle of Islam in respect of war and peace is given in these words of the Qur'an, `So long as they go straight with you, do go straight with them.' (9:7)

Patience, justice and recognition of limits are other essential attributes that Islam develops and wants to see activiated and acted upon in the believers. Islam warns the believers that if they have to take up arms they should not cross the limits set by Allah. The Qur'an says: 'if you punish, let your punishment be proportionate to the wrong that has been done to you. But if you are patient, it is certainly best for the patient. Be patient (then); and your patience is only by Allah's (help). Do not grieve for the unbelievers, nor distress yourself at their intrigues. Allah is with those who keep away from evil and do good (to others)' (16:126-28). It further says: 'O believers, be dutiful to Allah and bearers of just witness. Do not allow your enmity for others to turn you away from justice. Deal justly, justice is true piety. Have fear of Allah; He knows what you do.' (5:8). These teachings of patience and justice that are to be adhered to under all circumstances, also reflect in the strict conditions Islam puts to control and guide the conduct of war. Believers are asked to ensure the protection of women, children, old people, the non combatant among the civilian population, and members of the enemy forces in flight. They are told not to place any restrictions on the food supplies and water resources of the enemy. War in the modern sense, where there are no limits to violence and the aim is total destruction of the enemy by using the most savage devices and arms, has no sanction and acceptance in Islam.

Justice is the basic source of harmony and equilibrium in society. All violence and aggression have their origin in injustice. Where there is injustice; there cannot be peace and co-existence. Islam equates justice and peace. In the words of the Qur'an: 'O believers, conduct yourself with justice and bear true witness to Allah, even though it be against yourselves, your parents, or your kinsfolk.' (4:135).

The aforesaid makes it abundantly clear what the Qur'an fundamentally teaches and what the Prophet (PBUH) exemplified through his words and deeds, with regard to the questions of peace and war and violence. From the very concept and nature of Godhood to the conduct and character of the Prophet (PBUH), compassion and mercy are the most repeated defining qualities that characterize the kind of human person, attitude and behaviour Islam strives to build. Compassion and mercy lead to justice, fair play, patience, tolerance and co-existence. From the very beginning to the end, the Qur'an repeatedly impresses on its human audience to cultivate a positive attitude and shun all negativity. The Prophet is consistently insistent upon developing and promoting the moral and spiritual strength to return good for evil. All this stands to raise a Muslim as a model human being whose very presence extinguishes the raging fires of hatred and ill will and who acts as an abode of peace and security amidst a world torn apart by the animal drives of greed, selfishness, exploitation and domination. Such a purified and pacified human person cannot be the one who is abhorred today as a human bomb exploding and killing innocent human beings.

Such a person can be anything but a Muslim as he/she has no resemblance whatever to anything that Islam stands for. No matter how much they refer to and invoke Islam, Islam will always condemn them as transgressors of the limits set by Allah, the Compassionate, the Merciful and the Prophet who is a mercy to all mankind.

5

Islam and Co-existence in a Pluralistic Society

Religions have played the most important role in civilizing man by controlling his wild instincts and taming the beast in him. This miracle has been achieved by bringing him under the authority of a divine presence which is beyond him and also within him. All great religions attempted at metaphysical regeneration and enlargement of the human consciousness enabling man to outgrow his narrow and transient material existence and recognise the transcendent universality lying within it thereby paving the way for rendering him at peace with himself and also with other human beings.

But it is equally true that religions have also been the most powerful source of strife and confrontation among the followers. In spite of emphasizing almost similar human virtues these different religions gradually developed traits of exclusivism and xenophobia as they had emerged and grown in geographically secluded parts of the world. The followers of different religions, in course of time, became victims of "we" and "they" syndrome as they insisted more and more on their own religion being the only right path. The bigotry and fanaticism that are both the cause and effect of such an attitude thus prove to be the very undoing of the religions.

This attitude of exclusivism, however, became something very difficult to cope with in societies where followers of different religions happened to live together. In such societies, as most of the modern, democratic, economically mobile and pluralistic societies are, exclusivism can cause only alienation and isolation to its practitioner. A pluralistic society demands co-existence which is based on positive tolerance and respect for the other's identity. This naturally involves a broader and larger concept of God and man.

Now let us see what Islam has to offer in this context:

The very basis of Islam is peace. The word *Islam* is derived from the root *Silm* which means peace as also complete surrender to the will of the Creator. The Qur'an declares:

> "This day I have perfected your religion for you and completed My favour unto you and chosen for you as religion Al-Islam" (5:3)

This idea of peace has been extended to its logical culmination by the Quranic insistence on tolerance and peaceful co-existence. When the prophet was confronting the "Unbelievers" he did not quarrel with them. Instead, he was just asked to state what precisely was the difference between him and them and that each was entitled to his way: I do not want to force you to give up your way, you should not force me to give up mine.

The Qur'an enjoins:

> "Say, you who reject faith, I worship not that which you worship, nor will you worship that which I worship. And I will not worship that which you have been wont to worship. Nor will you worship that which I worship. To you your way and to me mine (109:1-6)"

And also:

> "Let there be no compulsion in religion. Truth stands out clear from error. He who rejects evil and believes in God has grasped the strong branch (of grace) which can not break. Remember God hears and knows all things" (2:256).

Islam enjoins on man to deal justly with all (*al-nas,* i.e., All mankind) and not merely his own coreligionists. Under no circumstances is unfairness to anyone, even the worst enemy, justified, for, according to the Qur'an "all mankind is a single community (*Ummah)*" (2:213) and the differences that divide them are either accidental or so that they may be 'recognised' as the Qur'an says:

> "If God had so willed, he could have made them a single people. But He admits whom He will to His grace: and for the wrong doers there will be no protector nor helper" (42:8)

> "Men, we have created you from a male and a female, and made you into nations and tribes that you might get to know one another. The noblest of you in Allah's sight is one who is most righteous of you. Allah is wise and All-Knowing" (49:13)

It has also been enjoined by the Qur'an that a Muslim should do good (*Ihsan*) not only to one's parents and relations but also to the orphans, the needy, the helpless, and the neighbour whether he is related to him in some way or not at all. This command is reinforced by a tradition of the Prophet, which says:

> A true Muslim is one who does no mischief to any other Muslim but "the true *Momin* (Man of genuine faith who is superior to a formal Muslim in merit) is one who does no mischief to his neighbours" and of whom they have no fear.

Here no distinction is made between a Muslim and a non-Muslim; all his neighbours should feel that there is not even a remote possibility of any evil coming to them from him.

The Qur'an again and again insists on its essential message of peace and commands the Muslims not to be led astray from the path of Allah in while dealing with their enemies.

It Commands:

> "And do not let your wrath against the people who have barred you from the Holy Mosque move you to commit undue transgression, rather, help one another in acts of righteousness and piety, and do not help one another in sin and transgression".

In another Quranic verse the principles of justice and fairplay are added to this theme. The Qur'an—says:

> "O ye who believe ! Be steadfast witness for Allah in equity and let not the enmity of any people move you to deviate from justice. Act justly, that is nearer to God-fearing...(5:8)

According to Qur'an a prophet is the 'universal man', par excellence. The prophet of Islam has been asked by the Qur'an to declare:

> "Say (O Muhammad): O Mankind! I am the messenger of Allah to you all (the messenger of) Him to whom belongs the dominion of the heavens and the earth (7:158)

and again:

> "We sent thee not save as a mercy for the people (21:107)

This means that the essence of the prophet's message—what the Qur'an calls the *Din*—is not addressed to any particular group or region or country but is meant for all mankind.

Now when the prophet of Islam has been sent to all mankind as a mercy, he must be acting as an uniting force building bridges amongst the people. The Qur'an declares that the prophet has brought the same message of Allah which other prophets had brought. It recognizes that all great religions point the same way to the attainment of truth, and their founders revealed its various facets and, therefore one must make no invidious distinctions between them. No other religion has stressed this revolutionary truth so repeatedly and forcefully. There are dozens of verses in the Qur'an which bring it out as an integral part of Islamic *anschauung:*

The Qur'an Says:

> "Say (O Muslims) we believe in Allah and that which is revealed unto us and that which was revealed unto Abraham and Ishmael and Isaac and Jacob and tribes and that which

> Moses and Jesus received and that which the Prophets received from their Lord. We make no distinction between any of them and unto Him we have surrendered (2:136).

> "Lo! Those who disbelieve in Allah and His messengers and seek to make distinction between Allah and his messengers and say: we believe in some and disbelieve in others and seek to strike a way between the two such are disbelievers in truth and for disbelievers we have prepared a shameful doom. But those who believe in Allah and His messengers and make no distinction between them, they will be given their rewards And Allah is ever Forgiving, Merciful, (4:150, 151, 152)

The Qur'an thus emphasizes that all the messengers of God have preached basically the same message, stressed the same values and they form the unbroken continuity of the eternal divine revelations. Speaking in the Quranic terminology it means that the *Din* (the basic spirit of religion) is the same while the *Shariah* (the ways to realise it in life) may differ. Nothing can, therefore be more imprudent than to ignore the unity underlying different faiths and start quarelling about the methods prescribed for the practice of the faiths. One of the great Persian Sufi poets, Jalaluddin Rumi, has expressed this truth in the following words.

> "I have picked up the esence from the Qur'an and thrown the bones for the dogs to quarrel over (*Diwan Shams Tabrez,* p. 546, Nawal Kishor Press, New Delhi)

This Quranic insistence on the essential unity of different divine revelations became the basis for peaceful co-existence of the people of different faiths. It also paved the way for the recognition and implementation of the rights of the non-Muslims living in an Islamic society. The prophet of Islam was so much concerned about the protection of the rights of the non-Muslims that he exhorted the Muslims: "Beware! On the day of judgment I will stand in appeal against anyone who commits excesses against any ally *(dhimmi)* or cuts short his rights or burdens him more than his endurance or receives anything from him without his consent (Abu Dawood—Kitab-al-Jihad).

The pious Caliphs, too, strictly followed the principles set by the Prophet (PBUH). During the time of the first Pious Caliph. Abu Bakr, a non-Muslim woman who abused Muslims had her teeth broken by some Muslims. On coming to know of the matter the Caliph wrote to his officer Mahajir bin Umayyah:

> "I have come to know that you have got two of the upper teeth of the woman who sang derogatory verses against Muslims, broken. A warning could be sufficient had she been a Muslim and her punishment must be less than a reprimand. Being a *Dhimmi* her singing these verses is nothing when her sin as great as the *shirk* is being tolerated. Had I been able to warn you earlier you must have tasted the punishment for your excess."

The second Pious Caliph Umar was so concerned about the treatment to the *Dhimmis* even at his death bed as he made the will:

> "I make this will for the Caliph replacing me that he must honour the agreement reached with the people whom the Prophet of Allah (PBUH) took under his protection, defend them and ensure that they are not burdened beyond their endurance."

The Islamic state is bound to honour, implement and protect the rights of the non Muslims and no Muslim has a right to tamper with or alter them as these are the rights enshrined in the Qur'an and the *Sunnah*. Muslims and non-Muslims are at par in an Islamic state from the stand point of the protection of rights. In a way non-Muslims enjoy an edge over the Muslims in matters of protection of these rights as the Islamic State may impose additional taxes on the Muslims or acquire their property under special circumstances but it can not overburden the *dhimmis* after the agreement with them is finalized.

The fourth Pious Caliph Ali stressed the same principles by saying "Do not reject any kind of peace and pact of co-existence to which your enemy invites you and in which there is Allah's satisfaction.... If you conclude an agreement with your enemy or undertake an obligation, be faithful to your pact and carry out your commitments in full honesty and make your life a guarantee for the protection of your obligations."

The provision of human rights to the non-Muslims or minorities under the Islamic system is based on the principles of justice, oneness of man and religious tolerance. It is said that any society is democratic only to the extent and measure it protects the rights of its minorities. Islam not only applied this yardstick but also institutionalised it.

The Prophet (PBUH) concluded many treaties and Tribute Agreements with people of different faiths living in Medina. The agreement concluded between the Prophet (PBUH) and the Christians of Sinai reads as follows:

> "...This is a writ according to which a treaty is concluded with them and whoever opposes its articles will be considered a transgressor to him and other Muslims. Such a person will be rejecting Allah's promise.... Whenever monks or travellers get together, and reside in the mountains or in the deserts, in an inhabited place or in plane, in synagogues or in temples, we will be behind them to preserve and protect them, and I will defend their lives, property and goods with my life and that of my friends, helpers and nation, since they are my subjects and united allies."

With the exception of what they willingly pay as tribute they will by no means be compelled to pay anything more or held responsible for it.

Their judges, monks, hermits and travellers will not be molested, and no synagogues or churches will be destroyed and nothing of their property may enter the Muslims' dwellings. (Ibn Hishm's Sirah. Vol. 2)

The above discussion can be summed up as follows:

1. Islam not only affirmed that there is truth in every religion but that all religions are true. It stated that the religion is God's gift to all mankind and it is, therefore, impossible that some groups should have received it and some should have been entirely deprived of it.
2. Islam advanced the view that even as the laws of nature regulated the machinery of the universe so was there a universal law which regulated man's spiritual development. The greatest error into which mankind has fallen was to forget this basic unity of God's religion and to divide mankind into rival groups, each at war with others.
3. The primary aim of religion was to remove the quarrel and dissentions corrupting the life of mankind and not to become itself a source of conflict. The great tragedy of man was that he turned an instrument of unity into a weapon of disunity.
4. The Qur'an made a significant distinction between religion and its outward observances. The former is called *Din* and the latter *Shariah* and *minhaj* (the way). *Din* was essentially one and the same everywhere and given to all without discrimination. But *Shariah* and *minhaj* naturally varied from time to time and from one people to another, depending on circumstances. But this difference in them could not alter the essential basis of religion. Men have forgotten the reality of religion and tend to deny the truth of other religions because they differ in their forms and ceremonies.
5. Islam made it clear that religious groupism and external forms have no part to play in the attainment of salvation and grace by man. The group formations are all man-made. The *Din* prescribed by God is but one.
6. Islam declared in clear terms that all religions are true. it is only their followers that have disregarded the truth

which they embody. If they return to their forgotten truth, the task of the Qur'an will be fulfilled.

7. Islam says that this *Din* of God was not meant to divide men from men but bring them together in a fellowship of love and to persuade them to live in unity bound together by the common tie of devotion to God. When there is one and the same God for all, when they are all bound in devotion to Him, when everyone has necessarily to reap what it sows, why should men fight one another in the name of God or religion?

This is the agenda Islam has set for co-existence in a pluralistic society. The world will become a much more civilised place to live if we ever choose to act upon it. But will we?

6

Islam and Science

Today Islam is being targeted by the most powerful combination of nations. It is accused of spreading the cult of terrorism, a kind of barbarism that, it is said should be fought out by civilized nations of the world. I am referring here to the astoundingly irrational thesis predicting that the world is moving inevitably towards 'Clash of Civilizations' when Islamic civilization will come in conflict with non-Islamic civilizations. I believe that the idea is prompted by mundane selfish interest of the sections to which Huntington belongs but I will not go into that here because we are having a discourse that will show how far it is from objective reality.

I come from a country whose preeminent leader of its struggle for national independence and first Prime Minister after independence, Jawaharlal Nehru, has paid fulsome tributes to the civilizing influence of Islam. In his book ***Glimpses of World History*** (published in mid-thirties of the last century), referring to the revolution that the Prophet (PBUH) wrought in the Arab life, Nehru wrote:

> "The story of Arabs and how they spread over Asia, Europe and Africa, and of the high culture and civilization which they developed, is one of the wonders of history."

And, in the following paragraph he explains the force that caused this wonder, saying:

> "Islam was the new force or idea which woke up the Arabs and filled them with self-confidence and energy."

The self-confidence was reflected in the Prophet sending out a message to the kings and rulers of the world to acknowledge the one God and His Prophet. Though most of the recipients of the message treated it with disdain, they could not keep their people from welcoming Islam because its message of brotherhood 'had a great appeal, not only for the Arabs, but also for inhabitants of many countries where they (the Arabs) went'. That was the main reason for the emergence of the vast empire that spread from the Atlantic in the West to the western border of the Indian sub-continent. That this self-confidence was not misplaced or irrational is evident from the fact that after Mohammad (PBUH) the world has not heard any other prophetic voice. That is why he is called the last Prophet, Nabi Aakhiruzzaman. Why is it so? Because the religion he preached provided scientific reasoning to the faith. Islam does not call for blind faith, it enjoins the study of the Qur'an (the revealed message) not without understanding but with deep insight. It has laid maximum emphasis on acquiring knowledge. It is now universally recognized that the literary, philosophical and scientific thought of Greece that had been practically lost to the western world were preserved and conveyed to Europe by the Muslim scholars who were enjoined to seek Knowledge 'even though it be in China'. The inspiration for incessant pursuit of knowledge, says Dr. K.G. Saiyidain, an eminent scholar and educationist, who was Education Advisor in the Ministry of Education, when Maulana Azad was the first minister in independent India, is directly attributable to the impulse provided by 'the teachings of the Qur'an and the Prophet'. He quotes the following verse of the Qur'an as evidence:

> "And God has brought you forth from your mothers' womb knowing nothing and He gave you ears and eyes and hearts so that you may show your gratitude."

How is gratitude shown if not by proper use of the gift. In

this case proper use would mean using the human faculties for promoting human welfare meaning thereby that if a person does not employ these faculties for the good of mankind he/she would be guilty of ingratitude to the Creator. The importance given by Islam to the pursuit of knowledge is evident in the following traditions of the Prophet (PBUH):

1. "God has revealed to me that whoever walks in the pursuit of knowledge, I facilitate for him the way to heaven. Increase in knowledge is even superior to increase in worship."
2. "The best form of worship is the pursuit of knowledge."
3. "Scholars should endeavour to spread knowledge and provide education to people who have been deprived of it. For where knowledge is hidden it disappears."
4. "Someone asked the Prophet who is the biggest scholar. He replied: 'He who is trying to constantly trying to learn from others, for a scholar is ever hungry for more knowledge.'"
5. Seek for knowledge and wisdom, whatever the vessel from which it flows. You will never be the loser."
6. "Thinking deep for one hour (with sincerity) is better than seventy years of (mechanical) worship."
7. "Worship without knowledge has no merit in it, and knowledge without understanding has no goodness in it. And the recitation of the Qur'an, which is not thoughtful has no merit in it."

What else is scientific approach if not this? Man has been designated by Islam as the 'noblest of creation'. Why? The answer has been provided by the great Islamic scholar *Mohammad Abduh* in his monumental work *Al-Tawhid* (Monotheism) (*which has been quoted* in *Islam aur Asr-e-Jadeed* Vol. III, No. 4) in the following words:

"Islam gave two great ideas to people which were tabooed to them at the time—absoluteness of personal will and freedom of opinion. They have helped in the (gradual) perfection of mankind and man learnt to actualize his potential capabilities. Some of the later European scholars are of the view that western culture and civilizations are essentially based on these two principles. Men learn to act (independently) and their minds to think and reflect correctly when people begin to realize their true worth and learn that they have the right to use their intellect in the search for truth and wisdom. They made this crucial discovery in the 16th century. One of these scholars has also recognized that the source of this intellectual illumination was the light of Islamic scholarship." This exercise of personal intellect is known as **Ijtihad**, which is responsible for the best developments in the history of Islam for, through this process, its concepts were brought in consonance with the new developments in social relations and phenomenon of nature. Sir Syed, (1817-1898) the great reformer and modernizer of Muslim mind, particularly in, Indian sub-continent, in 19th century when he founded Scientific Society and spearheaded the movement to attract Muslims towards modern education. His arduous struggle to fight the forces that were dead set against the reforms that he conceived has been lauded by one of his prominent political opponents, Maulana Abul Kalam Azad, in his convocation address at the Aligarh Muslim University in 1949 in the following words:

"It is difficult to realize the opposition and struggle which, a hundred years ago, faced the reformers (like Sir Syed) who wanted to introduce this new education in India… . The cry of religion supplied the opponents of progress with one of their most potent weapons. The path of religion is not in fact opposed to that of reason and knowledge but unfortunately this has often been represented to be so. "Human thought has had to face this conflict in different times in different countries. Europe went through this struggle in 17th and 18th centuries while the Eastern countries faced this struggle in the 19th century. Among the Muslims it took a longer time but in the end, the inevitable happened. His force of change triumphed and the new order had to replace the old. So far as the Muslims of India are concerned, one can assert without any fear of contradiction that the man who played the most important role in this struggle is the presiding spirit of this university. The battle was fought here in Aligarh and Aligarh is a visible embodiment of the victory of the forces of progress."

The contribution of that change is well reflected in the efforts of a leading Muslim entrepreneur in the field of Information Technology, Mr. Azim Premji. Remember that this is the field in which India is proud of being in the forefront of world development. Maulana Azad himself was a practitioner of this **Ijtihad** as he says in his *Tadhkirah* that "from the first day I have refused to be content with what my family, my education and my society gave me. I have never been bound by the patterns of tradition in any direction and the thirst for truth has never deserted me. There is no conviction in my soul which has not been subjected to all the conspiracies of disbelief." In his later work *Ghubar-i-Khatir* he has described how through the thorny desert of doubt he came to realize the significance of faith as the ultimate repose of the spirit. It is time for us to turn to the Qur'an how it has sought to release human intellect from the fetters of ignorance, conservatism, inertia and obscurantism. The Qur'an has repeatedly exhorted that it is incumbent on every human being to make full use of his/her intellectual capabilities in order to understand the world in which he/she is living and thus appreciate the significance of his relationship with fellow men and women and realize the power and glory of Allah through the study of Nature, which is the handiwork of God. The study is to comprise three particular areas which comprehend the whole field of knowledge. First of these is the 'Alam-i-Anfas' (world of man) in order to know how he works towards his destiny and how he goes astray and misses the destiny. The Prophet (PBUH) showed through his precepts and practices how a people can be released from ignorance and evil and transformed into 'the community of good' *(Khayr-i-ummah)*. In his own lifetime, he brought about a great revolution in the pattern of thought and conduct of people who came under his influence. It was these people who built a culture and civilization that Nehru called `the wonder of history'. The Prophet (PBUH) had released the hidden creative impulses of his followers which resulted in the flowering of a culture and civilization of extraordinary brilliance. His contribution is recognized even by western scholars. P.K. Hitti, for instance, says in his work, *Islam: A way of Life*:

> "It (Islam) holds the distinction of having been from the mid-8th century to the end of the 12th century unmatched in its brilliance and unsurpassed in its literary, scientific and philosophic output."

The second area of study prescribed is the *Alam-i-Afaaq* (the world of Nature). This is the source of all human and social sciences, which have grown in time both in their variety and scope. This area covers all that Nature connotes—the earth and the heavens, the seas and the mountains, the play of seasons, the rotation of days and nights and the plant and animal life. All the known sciences—geology, solar science, oceanology, meteorology, botany, zoology, biology etc., are the manifestations of this study. So are all the technologies-nuclear and others.

The third is the study of history (*Alam-i-Tarikh*) which shows that man, through his contact with his social and physical environment, developed great cultures and civilizations. Those who acted according to what Islam calls laws of God, i.e., compassion and justice which are the attributes of Allah, prospered. Those who transgress these *vital* principles and indulge in acts of inhumanity and injustice face the destruction of all the creation of his mind and creative skills. The Holy Qur'an says:

> "Many eras have passed before you. Go about, then, in the land and behold the end of those who gave the lie to (the directives and ordinances of Allah"

There are several verses in *Surah Al-Mominun* which dilate upon the importance of the study of these three domains of human concern. Verses 12 to 16 point to the need for reflecting upon the birth and growth of man and how he comes into full possession of his powers. The verses 17 to 22 deal with the world of Nature and how it has been designed to fulfil the needs of man and other living creatures. It is also pointed out how the earth, the sky, the rain, the fields and gardens, the cattle, the ships sailing on the seas have been made subservient to man so that he may use them for human welfare and progress. About 30 verses that follow refer to the history of ancient nations and cultures, which vanished because they failed to cultivate qualities for survival—not merely biological but also social and moral-necessary for a life with freedom and dignity. They split into warring groups sticking to their old beliefs and refusing to change according to the changing times. They were like dinosaurs that vanished because they could not adjust to the changes of time and clime. Islam's injunctions about knowledge and reason, the basis of scientific thought and development of research, are quite clear and explicit. In the heyday of Islam, the Muslim states and scholars enthusiastically followed these injunctions and made high level contributions to various sciences which created the civilization and culture that is the pride of Islam. It is now widely acknowledged that it was Islam that gathered scientific knowledge from all corners of the world and pulled Europe out of the darkness of ignorance and superstition. It was the impulse provided by Islamic scholars and scientists that led to European renaissance and after the 18th century they developed science and technology to further help the European states to dominate large parts of the globe. The Muslims remained content with their past glory and fell victim to the cramping influence of conservative Ulema who reduced the pursuit of knowledge to memorizing the Qur'an without understanding. This is what the Islamic social reformers and educational thinkers of the late 19th century onwards have been endeavouring to change. These reformers were at pains constrained to drive home the point to the opponents of modern education that they were wallowing in false pride in the past without any effort to make it a living reality in the present and future.

Let us now look at the achievements of the Muslims during the early centuries of Islam when the science policy aimed at gathering scientific knowledge from all over the globe. Scientific treatises of Greek, Byzantine, Persian, Indian and Chinese scholars were translated into Arabic so that the Arabs could have access to all the existing knowledge. The science policy was implemented, besides translation work on a gigantic scale, by setting up institutions for study and research. One such institution was ***Bait-ul-Hikmat*** that was founded by *Khalifa Mamoon* in 813 A.D. Before *Mamoon, Khalifa Haroon Rashid* had set up a similar institution ***Khazanat-ul-Hikma***. With these institutions were attached libraries and research laboratories. Missions were sent to various countries to collect scientific treatises. An outstanding example even of the *Ummayid* period is what *Mohammad bin Qasim* did after conquering *Sindh,* a remote north-western kingdom in the Indian subcontinent. Having known that the Indians had made great achievements in various disciplines of sciences as will as in mathematics, Muhammad bin Qasim, after the conquest of Sindh drifted Sanskrit Scholars rather than indulging in territorial expansion and took them with him to Damascus to help with translation of Indian scientific and mathematical treatises from Sanskrit to Arabic. These scholars were paid handsome remunerations for their work before they were repatriated. The respect that he had shown for their knowledge induced the people of the area to voluntarily convert to the religion of Islam. Thus, Muslim scientists were able to have a comprehensive view of the entire existing knowledge. Each scientist advanced the science of his natural preference beyond what he had learnt. A few names may be mentioned here to show how comprehensive was the knowledge of science in the early years of the advent of Islam. *Abu Yousuf Alkindi* known as *'Hakim-i-Arab'*, who lived during 9th century, was an original thinker. He wrote books on Mineralogy, Metallurgy, Geology, Physics and Pharmacology, besides philosophy and classification of knowledge. *Hunain bin Ishaque* was a leading figure among the school of translator scientists who had acquired mastery over Arabic, Syrian and Greek languages. He translated treatises from those languages and compared them in order to textualise the subjects. Apart from this work he made original contributions particularly in the field of medical research. *Abu Ali bin Al-Hasan ibn Al-Haitham* was a leading Mathematician and Physicist. About hundred names of his books have come to our generation. Of them 19 are currently being studied by scientists. His work has deeply influenced scholars in Europe where he is known as *Al-Hazen*. His contemporary, *Abu Rehan Al-Biruni* is considered by the well-known author Boplatt as the greatest scholar of the medieval period. *Al-Biruni* came to India along with *Mehmood Ghaznavi*. While the latter collected wealth from Indian temple treasuries, he amassed the vast wealth of science and literature. Towards this end, he learnt Sanskrit and translated various scientific and literary works into Arabic. Another unforgettable name is that of *Ibn-al-Shatir*, a resident of Syria, who was well-known as a master of planetary science. He is the father of Planetary Theory and invented instruments for observation and counting of the planets.

We have an idea of the dimensions in which Islamic scientists advanced human knowledge. Their outstanding contribution in the field of Mathematics is the invention of the decimal after the first nine digits, which took the place of zero, which was invented in India. *Abul Hasan Aqleedsi* has written a book in which there is an elaborate discussion on the use of decimal. *Al-Khwarizmi* wrote a book on Indian style of enumeration which was later translated into Latin. He is the originator of Algebra and the concept of Al-Logarithm has been associated with his name. Similarly important advances were made in the fields of Astronomy, and Chemistry, etc.

I would end this with the ideal that ***Sir Syed,*** the founder of my alma mater the Aligarh Muslim University, the first modern, secular institution in the world of Islam, put before the students of Mohammedan Anglo-Oriental College. It is relevant for every Muslim of modern age. He had said:

> "You should have Philosophy in the right hand, Science in the left, and on your head the Crown of the Kalima Tayyaba 'La Ilaha il-Allah, Mohammad Rasool-Allah'.

7

Citizenship and Minority Issues

A Quranic Perspective

In the rapidly globalising world today most of the countries are increasingly becoming cosmopolitan with people of different nationalities, religions, races, colours and languages coming together for various reasons. This religious, cultural and linguistic diversity is giving rise to the questions of the majority-minority relations which range from peaceful co-existence to violent confrontation and forced acceptance or passive toleration. In the countries having a long history like India where various minorities have been living side by side with the majority people. Muslims who have been here for about a millennium, have developed certain social, cultural and political characteristics that govern their relations with various minority groups as well as the majority, as a consequence of which, despite occasional conflicts, these relations remain more or less peaceful.

In other countries where various minorities are of recent or not too distant origin, their intermingling with the majority and acceptance in the dominant social milieu creates certain problems that sometimes find expression in the form of virulent xenophobia and violence. These uneasy majority-minority relations become all the more tense and volatile because of absence of relevant constitutional instruments determining human rights.

There is yet another aspect of the majority-minority relations that presents a queer scenario where a particular religious, racial, cultural or linguistic group is in the majority in a country but finds itself in a minority in the neighbouring one, like Muslims in Pakistan, Bangladesh and India, who coming from the same stock were divided about half a century ago.

There is one more minority situation, represented for example by the Muslims living in Europe or America, who are either permanent settlers having a long presence or recent and temporary immigrants who have migrated for economic reasons. Although covered and protected by strong legal and constitutional provisions, these minorities sometimes find themselves confronting situations of racial or religious prejudices that cause a lot of anguish and suffering to them, as is happening these days in various European countries.

But analyzing and commenting in detail on these majority-minority relations is beyond the purview of this paper that aspires to dwell at length on the Islamic view and perspective of minorities and the Islamic provisions for their protection and well-being.

Before embarking on this effort it would be appropriate to have a look at the fact that amidst all these conflicting expressions that responses to minorities are assuming in various countries, the saner elements have arisen to the need of arriving at a kind of consensus about the principles that should govern the relations with the minorities, and have initiated processes of dialogue at different levels-religious, cultural, racial, and political. This dialogue presupposes the overwhelming need of harmony and peace that are being increasingly felt as preconditions for development. Also with increasing and strengthening processes of democratization being witnessed in various countries, mostly in the developing world, a greater good sense seems to be prevailing both at governmental and public levels with regard to providing and protecting the minority rights, which in turn are perceived to be the defining features of a country's civilisational status.

Leaders and representatives of various religious traditions are actively engaged in promoting and strengthening this dialogue, completing and furthering the efforts being made by various U.N. agencies and other international institutions. The basic source and standard of human rights for the world today is the U.N. Universal Declaration of Human Rights adopted with the approval of all the members of this world body. As citizens of the world, Muslims also accept and follow this charter of human rights but they have another, more sanctified source of these rights and universal oneness of humanity in their own tradition and it is the Last Sermon of the Prophet of Islam.

Islam being the last revelation of the True Path from God almighty offers an answer to every question and resolution of all problems that the mankind may encounter. The divine source of Islamic guidance is vested in the holy Qur'an which is the eternal word of God. The Qur'an presents in all clarity all the guidance that human beings need to get the feeling of a well-being in this world and hereafter. The Qur'an also says that the Truth has been offered to all human beings through the last messenger of God. It claims its message to be the last and final word in the series of guidances revealed by God through His various prophets for all the peoples in the world and for all ages and places. But nowhere does the Qur'an compel a man/woman to accept its teachings, the acceptance or rejection depending entirely on the level of enlightenment and clarity of conscience one happens to achieve. This principle of non-compulsion has from the very beginning of Islamic history operated and was executed wherever Islam has been in power. Islam not only protected the human dignity of all the people, Muslim or non-Muslim, living under its jurisdiction, but also provided the minorities with all the rights that they could have.

Closely attached to the concern and responses about minorities is the acceptance and respect of the plurality and diversity of individual and collective human existence. The Qur'an has laid down a fundamental principle in this regard by saying:

> "Men, have fear of your Lord, who created you from a single soul. From that soul He created its mate, and through them He bestrewed the earth with countless men and women." (NISA: 1)

This verse clearly unfolds the nature of and pattern behind the scheme of creation by emphasizing that all human beings form one single family and the progeny of a common parentage. The other emphasis is on the fact that the various tribes and social groups, one finds in the world, are created by God Himself to establish different social and cultural identities. Islam accepts and respects this pluralism and diversity which also provides a guiding principle for tolerance in modern-day pluralist societies.

All human collectivities to survive physically and with all their religious, cultural, and linguistic identities intact need provision of basic conditions of life, which is another name of human rights as we understand them to day. Without these living-conditions having been ensured and protected no human group can even imagine to survive. Islam has very clearly and firmly laid down the principles that provide a basis for all human rights and enjoins its followers to abide and implement them. The first and foremost among these rights is undoubtedly the right to life. The Qur'an says that life is God's creation and nobody can deprive one of his/her right to life. It enjoins:

> "...and that you shall not kill—for that is forbidden by Allah—except for a just cause." (Anam-151)

The Qur'an is so particular in this matter that it blanketly forbids killing of human beings without a valid reason irrespective of creed, class or race. It says:

> "...whoever killed a human being, except as a punishment for murder or for sedition in the earth, should be looked upon as though he had killed all mankind; and that whoever saved a human life should be regarded as though he had saved all mankind." (*Al* 32):

> "...who slays a soul unless it be (in punishment) for murder or for spreading mischief on earth shall be as if he had slain all mankind; and he who saves a life shall be as if he had given life to all mankind."

It must again be stressed here that this Islamic provision of right to life is based not on any religious, racial or other sectarian considerations but entirely on human basis. All minorities living under the benign umbrella of an Islamic state enjoy this right. The prophet of Islam further explains this Islamic position by emphasizing that:

> "God has shut the doors of paradise to the one who kills a *Dhimmi*" (*aisai*)

A Hadith from Bukhari says that such a murderer will be deprived of even the fragrance of paradise.

The Qur'an in addition to the right to life also ensures protection of right to property saying that:

> "Do not usurp one another's possessions by false means, nor proffer your possessions to the authorities in order that you may sinfully or knowingly deprive others of a part of their possessions." (*Al-Baqarah* 188)

With the life and property having been ensured, a minority, especially the religious one, needs its freedom to religion and creed fully protected as no religious minority can survive with the religious freedom denied to it. Islam does not recognize any element of compulsion to be operative in matters of religion as it solely concerns a man's own freewill and conscience which are God's gifts to humanity. Islam is indeed based on the very realization that a man's religion or faith can never have a firm ground to stand upon unless it is based on a conscious, deliberate and willing choice. No amount of force or compulsion can ensure longevity and permanence of faith. The Qur'an has laid down the principle emphatically once and for all and for all times to come by declaring that:

"There is no compulsion in religion" (*Al-Baqarah*: 256)

The Qur'an further strengthens this position by asserting that if God had willed, He was powerful enough to make all human beings adopt Islam as faith but God has never willed so and instead leaves the matters of faith to individual conscience. Now when the Creator himself allows humans freedom of religion how can the creatures force someone to accept a particular faith. This principle of complete religious freedom has not remained a mere abstract theoretical formulation but one can witness it operating and executed throughout the history of Islam.

Hasan Basri, an eminent divine of mystic leanings of early Islam, wrote to the Caliph Umar bin Abdul Azeez: "The *ahl-e-Dhimma* (the protected people) enjoy freedom to follow their faith." (Sarakhsi, *al-Msoot:* 93.5) Imam Abu Yusuf has it in his *Kitab-al-Kharaj*: "Non-Muslims in an Islamic state enjoy freedom to blow their naqoos (conch-shells) and raise their crosses, except during the prayer times." (*Kitab-al-Kharaj*, 146, 147)

The third fundamental human right to be provided to the minorities relates to the provision of justice. With this right denied, no minority can live in peace and dignity as it will then have to face undue interference in its internal affairs. The Qur'an has laid firm grounds for provision of a climate where all the minorities enjoy justice and equality without any hindrance. It is so concerned about any breach of this principle that it says:

> "O believers, be upright bearers of witness for Allah. Do not let the enmity of any people move you to deviate from justice. Act justly; that is nearer to God-fearing and fear Allah; Surely Allah is well aware of what you do." (*Al-Maidah*: 8)

The Qur'an clearly enjoins its followers that all religious matters relating to the minorities must be settled on the basis of their religious texts and source of law. It says:

> "...let the followers of the Gospel judge by what Allah has revealed therein." (Al-Maidah: 47)

All these Quranic injunctions and provisions have been the basis for the emergence and flowering of a civilization that became the benchmark for all the excellence the mankind is capable of performing and achieving in shaping the socio-cultural, economic, political and moral life of human collectivities. This has not been a hollow claim but was always accompanied by concrete action that created a polity where the minorities were accorded the right to life, property, movement, economic activity, profess, practice and propagate religion, adjudicate their personal laws according to their religious provisions, get justice, establish and run their system of education, protest against excesses, express views, get employment, build and safeguard their collective identity and lead a life of dignity.

The Prophet of Islam, after coming to Madina, established an elaborate system that ensured protection of all the civil and political rights of the minorities. This system was based on bonding all the religious and cultural entities living at Madina into a single and composite social identity, actuated by solemnizing a formal pact called 'Madina Covenant' (Meesaq-e-Madina). Under this Pact the entire Madinan society, including Christians and Jews, was termed as a single composite social collectivity. The Christians, Jews and other minority groups were given the right and the freedom to remain on their religion and conduct their religious affairs as they wished. They were called upon to defend along with others the land and society in the face of any aggression. The 'Madina Pact' is a glorious Islamic legacy that has served and can still serve as a model of peaceful co-existence in a plural society because it contains not only theoretical formulations but also practical endeavours to found and sustain a social structure which accommodates its diverse constituents and gives them their due.

Another source of Islamic glorification of human unity, dignity, equality and equity is the Last Sermon of the Prophet that he delivered on the occasion of the last Hajj that he performed. It can be said with certainty and without any fear of contradiction that the principles of human unity and equality enunciated in this Sermon some fourteen centuries ago, laid the foundations of what we see today in the form of UN Declaration of Human Rights. The Sermon declared before a huge congregation of the faithful that all human beings are equal with no one having an edge over the other as all are the progeny of Adam and Adam was made of clay; that every one's life is protected and the murderer will be done to death in return; that every one's property is protected; that usury is prohibited as it serves a very dangerous source of exploitation of the weak in the hands of the powerful; everyone is innocent before his/her crime is proved and nobody can be arrested without committing a crime; that the rights of the weaker sections of society are protected and as such women enjoy equal rights as men; that the rights of the subordinates are protected and they have to be provided with the same food and clothings as one has for oneself.

In the light of the above discussion on the Islamic view and practice of human rights one thing can be safely generalized that most of the ills that beset and plague the world today and the entire world system are because of the denial of rights and justice to a large part of the humanity by a few countries that have monopolized all the power and resources and are unabashedly trying to impose their, will and exploitative domination on the rest of the world by the so-called Third World which inspite of having 90 per cent of the entire world population, are forced to remain in a state of abject poverty and virtual slavery.

This is high time that all the Muslims in the world come forward to present to the world an actualisation of what Islam has been and has contributed to the building of a grand civilization and how this miracle can be repeated through exemplifying the Islamic teachings in their individual and collective lives. This is the only way the sinister machinations to present Islam and Muslims as sources of terrorism can be successfully countered and neutralized.

8

Islam and Minority Rights

Since man started leading sedentary life efforts have been on to define the nature and limits of human social behaviour. It has been necessary because, without imposing an order on human behaviour and social relations, it was impossible to create conditions of peace in society for without peace the very human existence, let alone the stability of the social structure, could be in peril. Various principles, laws and theories have been put forward in different societies and times to bring human behaviour under the protective control of reason rather than letting these be swayed by wild instincts so that human beings could outgrow their selfish concerns and recognize the existence and interests of the people other than themselves.

But history bears witness to the fact that despite these efforts by the prophets, saints and thinkers in almost all societies and times human relations have more or less been defined by suppression and repression. Normally human beings have been divided in the categories of the strong and the weak with the weak through a thorough psychological conditioning resigning themselves to accepting their plight without any protest. In the circumstances the very concept of human rights was irrelevant. The same was true of the rule of law.

All this however, changed forever with the advent of Islam. Islam, by bringing human beings under the authority of one God, freed them from the humiliation of prostrating before other human beings like themselves as now there was a divine presence which pervaded everything. The idea of one God paved the way for the emergence of justice leading to recognition of human rights.

The division between 'us' and 'they' based on the allegiance to a particular creed, race or colour has always been there. Islam did away with this division by recognising, establishing and protecting the basic human rights of all the people in the Islamic society irrespective of caste, creed and colour. The provision of human rights to non-Muslims or minorities under the Islamic system is based on the principles of justice, oneness of man and religious tolerance. It is said that any society is democratic only to the extent and measure it protects the rights of its minorities. Islam not only applied this yardstick but also institutionalised it to the extent that the Prophet of Islam, while showing concern for the protection of the rights of non-Muslims, exhorted: "Beware! On the day of Judgment I will stand in appeal against anyone who commits excesses against any ally (*dhimmi)* or cuts short his rights or burdens him more than endurance or receives anything from him without his consent *Abu Dawood Kitab-al-jihad*.

The Prophet concluded many treaties and Tribute Agreements with different people. The agreement concluded between the Prophet and the Christians of Sinai went as follows:

> "...This is a writ according to which a treaty is concluded with them and whoever opposes its articles will be considered a transgressor to him (the Prophet) and other Muslims. Such a person will be rejecting Allah's promise...
>
> "...Whenever monks or travellers get together, and reside in the mountains or in the desert, in inhabited places or in planes, in synagogues or temples, we will be behind them to preserve and protect them, and I will defend their lives, property and goods with my life and that of my friends, helpers and nation, since they are my subjects and united allies.
>
> "With the exception of what they willingly pay as tribute

> they will by no means be compelled to pay anything more or held responsible for it.
>
> "Their judges, monks, hermits and travellers will not be molested and no synagogue or church will be destroyed and nothing of their property may enter the Muslims' dwellings" (*Ibn Hisham's Sirah*. Vol. 2)"

The Righteous Caliphs, too, strictly followed the principles set by the Prophet (PBUH). During the time of the first Pious Caliph Abu Bakr a non-Muslim woman, who abused Muslims, had her teeth broken by some Muslims. On coming to know of the matter the Caliph wrote to his officer Mahajir Bin Umayyah:

> "I have come to know that you have got two of the upper teeth of the woman who sang derogatory verses against Muslims, broken. A warning could have been sufficient had she been a Muslim and her punishment must be less than a reprimand. Being a *dhimmi* her singing these verses is nothing when her sin as great as the Shirk is being condoned. Had I been able to warn you earlier you must have tasted the punishment for your excess."

The second Righteous Caliph Umar was so concerned about the treatment to the *dhimmis* that even on his death bed he made the will:

> "I make this will for the Caliph succeeding me that he must honour the agreement reached with the people whom the Prophet of Allah (PBUH) took under his protection, defend them and ensure that they are not burdened beyond their endurance".

The Islamic state is bound to honour, implement and protect the rights of the non-Muslims, and no Muslim has a right to tamper with or alter them as these are the rights established and ordained by the Qur'an and the Sunnah, Muslims and non-Muslims are at par in an Islamic state from the standpoint of the protection of rights. In a way non-Muslims enjoy an edge over the Muslims in this regard as the Islamic state may impose additional taxes on the Muslims or acquire their property under special circumstances but it can not overburden the *dhimmis* after the agreement with them is finalised.

In the Islamic state the civil and penal laws of Islam are equally applicable to the non-Muslims except with regard to the consumption of alcohol. According to Imam Malik, they enjoy exemption even with regard to fornication. Non-Muslims are free to brew, drink and sell wine among themselves and to keep, eat and sell wines among themselves. The Islamic State allows the personal matters of the non-Muslims to be adjudicated by their Personal Laws. Khwaja Hasan Basri decreed, on a query from the Caliph Umar Bin Abd-al-Aziz:

> "They have consented to pay *Jizya* on the condition that they will be granted freedom to lead their lives according to their faith. You must follow the established path and not invent any new way."

Non-Muslims are also free to arrange for the education of their children the way they like, establish educational institutions and propagate their religion among themselves.

In view of the provision of such rights for the non-Muslims under the Islamic system and tradition, the accusations of intolerance and fanaticism levelled against Islam by certain quarters and a section of the media are unfortunate. Equally unfortunate is the behaviour of those Muslims who show aggressive narrow-mindedness and intolerance towards non-Muslims and their cultural expressions. Both the attitudes do gross injustice to Islam. In the circumstances, those Muslims who consider Islam's message of universal humanism the basis of their identity have a greater much more responsibility. The world of today needs the enlightenment of the original spirit of Islam much more than ever before as the darkness has also grown thicker and multilayered.

9

Muslim Non-Muslim Relations

Principles and Application

Pluralism and co-existence are the two fundamental manifestations of the divine scheme of things unfolding through the harmony and balance that characterize and sustain the cosmos. All the celestial bodies inhabiting the universe, though strangers to each other, live in perfect balance, moving in their given trajectories. Our planet earth, that forms 'a tiny speck of dust' of the incredibly vast cosmos, is home to an unimaginable variety of living beings belonging to plant and animal kingdoms; all living independently and together, sustaining each other and respecting each other's space of existence.

However, human beings have been the only living beings who have consistently shown the tendency of dishonouring and violating the divine dispensation of pluralism and co-existence. The history of human civilization stands witness to the uncomfortable fact that the more various religions, divine messages and ethical preachings have tried to prevail upon man by taming his animal instincts to bring him within the boundaries of civilization, the more the human race has fought with each other on the basis of creed, culture, colour, and race, trying to dominate by denying others the right to exist. One reason for this state of perpetual strife and conflict, that characterizes the entire human history, has been the xenophobia—the fear of the other—the stranger which found its way in the collective psychologies of various human groups as geographical distances made them remain mutually exclusive. In the circumstances, word of mouth, received opinions, preconceived notions and stereotypes were the only sources of information about each other which always painted the other in horribly dark colours, to be feared and warded off.

Things started changing with the advancements in science and technology. The second half of the twentieth century undoubtedly was an unprecedented era in the human history which saw phenomenal growth in the means of transport and communications, leading to a radically massive transformation of the world that has rendered all its previous and up-till-now prevalent images redundant and irrelevant. Advances in communication and information technology have done away with geographical distances and squeezed the entire world into what is called a global village. All the information about any subject under the sun can now be accessed on one's laptop. This information boom, together with the explosion of the mass media, has created an environment where, the concept of the 'other' is no more relevant, at least in principle, as in the global market-place of information all the peoples, societies, cultures, races, languages and religions are allowed to speak for themselves and nobody who cares to listen can afford to remain unaware about others. In this global trend towards universalism, pluralism has regained its lost value and co-existence is being recognized as the only way of life available to humankind, if it chooses to survive.

But this does not mean that the world is now free from strife and conflict. In fact, the knowledge boom has brought in its wake a peculiar kind of ignorance that rejoices in exclusivism and refuses to accept pluralism and co-existence as norms of civilized human behaviour. Religion, unfortunately again, seems to be one of the sources of conflict. And doubly unfortunate is the fact that the religion being misused and misrepresented the most is Islam, which ironically in essence is the religion of peace and co-existence.

Islam is the most talked about religion in the world today,

thanks to certain acts of violence that have the dubious distinction of being linked and referred to it. The media, mainly western, the world over, is engaged in intensifying these links to convince the world that Islam and Muslims believe in dividing mankind into 'us' and 'they' and insist on eliminating all 'others'. It is in the context of this unjust and unkind campaign of disinformation, that a humble attempt is made here to highlight the kind of relationship that Islam enjoins the Muslims to have with non-Muslims which in essence is based on peace, tolerance and co-existence.

Islam, as we all know, is the latest version of the divine guidance to the mankind revealed through a chain of prophets. Being a compendium of all the values and virtues contained in the previous divine guidance, Islam's revealed book, the holy Qur'an, is addressed to all mankind and not to Muslims alone.

And the messenger of Islam, the Prophet Mohammad (PBUH) is described by the holy Qur'an as the one, who has been sent to all mankind as a mercy which reflects the two fundamental attributes of Allah, the beneficence and mercifulness. Such a Prophet (PBUH) cannot be expected to harbour any ill-will against human beings, Muslim or non-Muslim. And the Prophet (PBUH), through his words and deeds, exemplified that in all human affairs, all human beings are equal.

Islamic teachings on Muslim non-Muslim relations can be Summed up in the following principles:

HUMAN DIGNITY

Allah has made man the most exalted and loftiest of all creatures. He is not only superior to all other creatures but everything on the earth and in the skies has been made subservient to and put into service of mankind. All human beings equally share this honour irrespective of creed, colour or race. As the holy Qur'an says, 'And we have honoured the offspring of Adam' (*Al-Isra*:20) and 'We created man with the noblest image' (*Al-Teen*: 4) and no human being can be slighted or made a target of violence on the basis of religion or any other material consideration.

There are many instances in the life of the Prophet (PBUH) which recognize this essential exaltedness of mankind without any trace of discrimination on the basis of religion or creed. Once the dead body of a Jew was being carried in front of the Prophet (PBUH). The Prophet (PBUH) stood up in respect on which some of his companions asked him, 'O Prophet of Islam! It was the dead body of a Jew.' The Apostle of Allah replied, 'he too is a human being.' (*Muslim*). The message is clear: A human being is honourable just because of being human, irrespective of the religion he professes.

The holy Qur'an emphasizes the human dignity by calling the entire mankind as one extended family. It says, 'Men! have fear of your Lord, who created you from a single soul. From that soul He created its mate, and through them He bestrewed the earth with countless men and women.' (Al-Niṣa:1). This holy Quranic verse makes clear that all human beings are members of one human family and so are brothers and sisters to each other. And as this kinship is based on purely human grounds, not only Muslims but all humans professing any religion or creed are brothers and sisters to each other. This is the fundamental Islamic exposition of universal human fraternity, enunciated long before the French Revolution issuing the famous slogan of 'Liberty, Equality and Fraternity' and the adoption of the Universal Declaration of Human Rights by the UNO.

SECURITY OF LIFE, PROPERTY AND HONOUR

The second Islamic principle, basic to Muslim non-Muslim relations, concerns the sanctity and security of life, property and honour of all humans, irrespective of creed or religion. Islam ensures and guarantees security to life, property and honour of all human beings professing any religion.

For Islam, human life is sacrosanct. Killing a human being without any reason is just unacceptable to Islam. Under Islamic dispensation, the life of all Muslims is secure and so is the case with the non-Muslims. The Apostle of Allah (PBUH) says: 'the blood, property and honour of every Muslim is inviolable to any other Muslim' and the holy Qur'an ordains: 'whoever killed a human being, except as a punishment for murder or for sedition on earth, should be looked upon as though he had killed all mankind; and that whoever saved a human life should be regarded as though he had saved all mankind.' (*Al-Maidah*:32). This Quranic verse does not make any distinction on the basis of religion as its appeal is universal. The Prophet (PBUH) has expressly declared that the security of life is indivisible and is an inalienable right of all humans, irrespective of creed or religion. He says: 'Their (non-Muslims) blood is like our blood and their property is like our property.'

The concept of human life being sacrosanct and inviolable finds expression in the principle of life for life having been made applicable to Muslims and non-Muslims, equally. So, as the murderer of a Muslim is punished with death, the Muslim murderer of a non-Muslim will also meet the same fate. Islamic history is replete with the instances of Muslims receiving death penalty for killing non-Muslims. The Apostle of Allah (PBUH) was so particular and insistent in this regard that he had to say: 'Anyone who kills one of the people of agreement (read a non-Muslim) will never feel the fragrance of paradise while this fragrance will be felt from a distance of a 40 mile long walk.' (*Al-Bukhari*: Hadith no. 3166). In Islam, price of life is equal for Muslims and non-Muslims. So if the kin of the slain person forgives the murderer and agrees to accept the compensation, the amount of compensation will be the same for Muslims and non-Muslims.

Property is equally inviolable both in the case of Muslims as well as non-Muslims. The holy Qur'an exhorts: 'Believers! Do not consume your wealth among yourselves illegally' (*Al-Nisa*:29). The Prophet was so concerned about any excess and ill-treatment against non-Muslims that he reprimanded the believers: 'Take it from me that if anyone among you torments any of the 'people of agreement' or violates his right or burdens him more than he can endure or takes away anything from him without his consent, then on the Day of Judgement I would be on the side of that man.'

The same is the case with the security of honour where also Islam does not draw a line between Muslims and non-Muslims.

RELIGIOUS FREEDOM

Islam allows complete freedom of choice in matters of religion or creed. No human being can be forced to accept any faith which depends on an individual's level of consciousness and attitude. The holy Qur'an long ago enunciated the fundamental principle of religious freedom by saying: 'There is no compulsion in religion.' And the Qur'an is so strict in this matter that it does not allow even its Apostle (PBUH) to force anyone to accept Islam. It says: 'Will you force the people into believing.' The Qur'an sums up the entire disputation on religion by announcing that 'To you your religion, to me mine.' (*Al-Kafiroon*: 6)

KINDNESS AND COOPERATION

The fourth cardinal Islamic teaching on Muslim non-Muslim relations refers to the values of kindness and cooperation towards each other, irrespective of creed or religion. The Prophet (PBUH) enunciates the principle in these words: 'God, the Beneficent has mercy on those who treat others kindly; be kind to those on earth and the Lord of skies will have mercy on you.' (*Al-Tirmizi*). He re-emphasizes the same point by saying: 'One who does not have kindness for others, does not receive kindness.' (*Al-Bukhari*) The Apostle of Allah (PBUH) has repeatedly stressed the value of mutual cooperation. One of the Prophetic Traditions has it: 'All the creatures are Allah's family and the one of this family is dearest to Allah who treats His family well and kindly." (*Mishkaat*).

SOCIAL RELATIONS

On the basis of the above-mentioned principles Islam enjoins the Muslims to have social relations with the non-Muslims without any prejudice and discrimination. These relations should be characterized by sympathetic behaviour, ethical principles and justice. The holy Qur'an lays down a fair principle for these relations. It says: 'Allah does not forbid you to be kind and equitable to those who have neither made war on your religion nor driven you from your homes. Allah loves the equitable.' (*Al-Mumtah nai*: 8).

Relations with non-Muslims cover all social intercourse including sharing each other's joys and sorrows, mutual help in need and cooperation in social reconstruction, welfare programmes and promotion of knowledge and education. The Apostle of Allah (PBUH) accepted invitations from non-Muslims and invited them. He had non-Muslim guests at his home and treated them with exemplary kindness. Islam puts great emphasis on treating the neighbours well, respecting their rights and helping them in need. Here again, no distinction is made between a Muslim and non-Muslim. The Prophet (PBUH) calls upon the Muslims to be sensitive, caring and helpful to those in distress, the ailing and the needy. He himself visited the ailing non-Muslims and tried to console them in every possible manner. Muslims have been enjoined to wholeheartedly engage in rescue and relief work whenever any natural calamity or man-made disaster strikes. The Islamic principle in this regard is: 'He is the best among human beings who is the most beneficial to humans.' The Prophet (PBUH) has laid great stress on mingling with the people and enduring the sufferings it brings. According to a Hadith: 'A believer who participates in the affairs of other people and endures with patience the sufferings it brings is better than the believer who does not mingle with others and refuses to bear with patience the sufferings it brings.'

Islam does not allow the religious differences to come in the way of promotion of knowledge and education. It permits the Muslims to receive education from non-Muslims and promote education among them. To the Apostle of Allah (PBUH) 'Knowledge is the lost treasure of a believer.' (Tirmizi: 2687) and a believer should strive to get knowledge from whatever source it comes, no matter how far one has to travel to get it. The Prophet (PBUH) set an example in this regard when after the battle of Badr he asked non-Muslim prisoners who knew reading and writing to teach ten residents of Madina to read and write and earn freedom. This was the only school in the entire Islamic history where all the teachers were non-Muslims and all the students Muslim.

ECONOMIC RELATIONS

Islam believes in uninterrupted economic relations with non-Muslims as it recognizes the necessities of a plural society where people of different religions cannot survive without economic cooperation. The Prophet (PBUH) himself had economic relations with non-Muslims; Jews especially with the His companions also followed suit. The fourth Righteous caliph, Hazrat Ali served a Jew as a labourer. Non-Muslims, too, were employed by the Muslims for various services. The Prophet (PBUH) took a non-Muslim on a journey to show the way and paid him for the job. There are many instances in Islamic history of non-Muslims occupying high offices in the courts of Muslim rulers.

Another important aspect of these relations is that Islam exempts the non-Muslims from certain economic rules and regulations. Rules regarding the usury which is completely prohibited for the Muslims do not apply to non-Muslims. Muslims have been enjoined to be fair and just in their dealings with non-Muslims.

POLITICAL RELATIONS

Islam has provided a clear guidance in respect of the political relations the Muslims need to have with non-Muslims in a Muslim society. Madina was a plural society with Christians, Jews and other non-Muslim groups sharing the social space with the Muslims. The Prophet of Islam (PBUH) who was wedded to the principles of peace and harmony had to set an example of political relations with the non-Muslim groups who were the minorities in the Islamic society at Madina. As it was impossible for Muslims not to come into contact and interact with non-Muslims, in day-to-day social matters, certain principles had to be devised in order to guide and direct this interaction. It was also apprehended that Muslims being in a majority might tend to impose their collective will on the non-Muslims and dominate them in a manner that negates the very essence of Islamic message of universalism. Thus the Prophet (PBUH) came forward with the idea of concluding agreements with the non-Muslims seeking to provide them all the rights, freedoms and protections that the minorities must enjoy. So many agreements were concluded by the Prophet (PBUH) with various groups of *ahlul Kitab* (people of the Book). Here is the text of the agreement concluded between the Prophet and Christians of Sinai, which shows how much the Prophet (PBUH) was concerned with the rights and security of the non-Muslims.

In the name of Allah, the Beneficent, the Merciful. This is a letter written by Muhammad, son of Abdullah, as a bearer of good news and a warner, and in respect of Allah's trust, entrusted with all creatures, so that no plea would be made to Allah after the Prophet (PBUH). Allah Almighty is Wise.

He has written this to those who follow his faith as a treaty with the groups of the east and west who are Christians, be they near or far, Arab or non-Arab, known or unknown. This is a writ according to which a treaty is concluded with them, and whoever opposes its articles will be considered a transgressor to him and other Muslims. Such a person would be rejecting Allah's promise by not being honest nor humble in his agreement, ridicule his own religion and so deserving damnation, be he a king or an ordinary Muslim believer.

Wherever monks or travellers get together, and reside in the mountains or in the deserts, in inhabited places or in planes, in synagogues or temples, we will be behind them to preserve and protect them, and I will defend their lives, property and goods with my life and that of my friends, helpers and nation, since they are my subjects and united allies.

With the exception of what they willingly pay as tribute they will by no means be compelled to pay anything more or held responsible for it.

Their judges, monks, hermits and travelers will not be molested, and no synagogue or church will be destroyed and nothing of their property may enter the Muslims' dwellings.

Judges and monks are exempt from paying tribute, so are those engaged in the task of worship.

The wealthy and men of commerce should not be required to pay anything in excess of their tribute.

"None of them will be forced to fight or carry arms.

"Rather the Muslims should defend them, and converse with them in the best manner and according to the holy verse which says:

Do not argue with Ahlal-Kitab except in the best manner. (Al-Ankabut:46)

They may live in a safe environment which is full of kindness, and everything is to be done to check what may cause them annoyance and uneasiness, wherever they may be and wherever they may reside.

This agreement is signed by the Holy Prophet (PBUH), and undersigned by a number of his friends as witnesses. (*Ibn Hisham's Sirah*, Vol. 2, p. 902)

The following treaty, too, was concluded between the Prophet and Yuhanna, son of Rubah, chief of the Christians of Ila (*al-Aqabah*):

In the name of Allah, the Beneficent, the Merciful. This is a guarantee on behalf of Allah and Muhammad, his Messenger given to Yuhanna, son of-Ru'bah, and the people of Ila, according to which their ships and travellers are under the protection and security of Allah and His Messenger, and all their companions from ash-Sham, Syria or on the coasts of the sea are immune and under protection.

Elements causing incidents will never be exempted from trial because of their wealth, and if they are captured they will be considered as slaves.

It is forbidden to prevent access to water-springs to them (People of Ila) or bar them from proceeding on their way either by land or by sea.

This treaty is written by Juhayn, son of as-Salt Serjil, son of Hasnah with the permission of the Messenger of Allah.

Another treaty with the people of Najran goes as follows:

"In the name of Allah, the Beneficent, the Merciful.

This is a treaty concluded by the Messenger of Allah and the people of Najran. Their agricultural products and property will be protected and the whole will be returned to them. They will pay two thousand suits of clothes annually, one thousand of which must be delivered in the month of Ramadan, and the other thousand in the month of Safar. If there is an increase or decrease of crops, they will be evaluated according to measure. Other products of theirs such as war garments, horses, livestock and other war equipments will be received on the basis of calculation.

The people of Najran undertake to host the envoys of the Messenger of Allah for a month or less, but not for more than one month. If a plot is hatched in Yemen, the people of Najran lend thirty war equipment, thirty horses and thirty camels to reinforce the Muslims, and if any of this number is lost or damaged, the Muslims must restore it by paying the equivalent.

Najran and its neighbourhood will be under Allah's

protection and will be bound by the pact of Muhammad, the Messenger of Allah, together with its people, its territory, property, the present or the absentees, its travellers, delegates and temples. No change will be made in their condition, and no rights of theirs will be altered. Their temples remain intact, and their bishops, monks and church adherents as well as what they possess will not be molested, and no imposition will be made on them. They are exempt from the blood money of the pre-Islamic period. They will not be called to account nor are they required to pay one-tenth tax. Their territory will not be occupied by Muslim troops. Those who appeal for justice will be treated with equity and justice. In Najran, there will remain no oppressor nor oppressed. Those who continue to engage in usury will receive no protection, whatever. No person will be held responsible for another person's fault.

According to this treaty the people of Najran will be protected by Allah and Muhammad, His Messenger, till the Day of Judgement, and so long as they do not deviate from the highway of benevolence and peacefulness, no imposition on them and no injustice will be made towards them.

RELIGIOUS RELATIONS

Religious relations with non-Muslims have been characterized in Islam by the principles of perfect non-interference and tolerance. As has been mentioned earlier, the holy Qur'an has enunciated two clear principles to serve as a basis for non-interference and tolerance. These principles contained in two Quranic verses which announce: *'There is no compulsion in Islam'* and *'To you your religion and to me mine.'* did not remain as mere intellectual assertions in the Islamic societies but were put into practise and institutionalized as far as possible. Places of worship of non-Muslims were protected and their personal laws made inviolable through a policy of non-interference by the Muslim rulers.

No doubt Muslims have been asked to maintain their

distinct Islamic identity as they are not supposed to get assimilated into the non-Muslim society nor should they try to assimilate the non-Muslims into their own.

This was a brief account of the principles and practice of Muslim and non-Muslim relations the holy Qur'an and the gracious Prophet of Islam (PBUH) have set and made incumbent upon all the Muslims to follow. These principles and practices equally apply to all the Muslims whether they form a majority in an Islamic society or a minority in a society with a non-Muslim majority. In a Muslim society, they are called upon to respect and protect the rights provided and guaranteed by Allah and His Messenger to the non-Muslim minorities and treat them humanely and according to the essence of the Islamic message of universal human brotherhood. Where Muslims are in a minority they have Islamic guidance to zealously cooperate with their non-Muslim compatriots in all activities involved in social reconstruction and general welfare of the people. In case their rights are violated, freedoms curtailed and they are made targets of political repression, they have every right to protest but within the limits of peace and civilized decency set by Islam.

These Islamic principles for guiding relations with non-Muslims were obviously laid down when Muslims were socially and politically dominant which means that Islam was the first religion to recognize the existence of religious minorities and their rights and make provisions and provide guarantees for their protection and well-being. It is now upto Muslims to uphold these principles, in word and deed, to reinforce the truth that Islam has been a civilizing force in human history and it is so even today, against all efforts to present it in an image totally contrary to its essence.

10

Islam and Religious Pluralism

We are now witnesses to a globalizing world. Rapid and mind-boggling advances in the field of communication and information technology have squeezed our planet into what is called a global village where not only distances have shortened but also people around the globe have come together in a way that someone in one part of the world can feel the living presence of someone sitting thousands of kilometers away by just a click of a computer mouse. People now know much more about each other than ever before. No era in human history has seen such an abundance of knowledge and explosion of information as our age has. Newspapers, electronic media and above all the great internet have opened up our eyes and minds to a new world of possibilities and of knowing about the customs and traditions, religion and culture of the people who have hitherto been complete strangers to each other.

This technology-driven squeezing of the world has also brought in its wake another phenomenon which is unprecedented in its magnitude and scale. I am referring to the growing interlinking and inter-dependence of the people the world over. Knowing about each other's society, culture, faith and religion has now moved beyond a mere academic interest to become an inevitable human need. As the world grows into a theatre of cultural intermingling, people of various social and cultural milieus, faiths and religions are bound to be more and more closely informed about each other, if they wish to cope with the tide of growing interdependence. No cultural or religious group can afford to remain isolated from the other. Exclusivism is making way for an all-inclusive acceptance of others. In fact the unfolding postmodern scenario will soon leave no space for the 'other'.

The last century had seen people from one part of the world moving out of their places and migrating to other parts of the world on an unprecedented scale, more notably in various European countries, U.S.A. and the Gulf region. It has resulted in rendering these places into hubs of socio-cultural intermingling. These socio-cultural and economic processes soon attracted the attention of the academics who were eager to understand and define this new phenomenon and its cultural and political fall-out. Thus two terms—multi-culturalism and pluralism—were coined and came into vogue. Both these seemingly interlinked terms seek to define the presence of people belonging to diverse nationalities, social and cultural milieus and faith; backgrounds in a society which has so far been predominantly mono-cultural and mono-religious. With the passage of time, however, the term pluralism has got an edge over multi-culturalism as the former has proved itself to be much more comprehensive and inclusive.

As the world is struggling hard to revive its multi-polarity at the political plane, the movement towards strengthening of a thoroughly pluralist society at the global level is also gaining momentum. Such a globally pluralized social and cultural system would, however, spring certain uncomfortable questions to various religions, especially the missionary ones like Islam and Christianity. These religions, while trying to come to terms with these questions, would have to make difficult choices for striking necessary adjustments in a pluralist social and cultural reality. Would these religions be able to make adjustments within the framework of pluralism? Do these religions have any bases in their core teachings and value system that might help them in this process of adjustment and accommodation? Answers to these questions are increasingly important as the world today is heavily banking on religious resources and core religious values in its search for ways and means to resolve the problems relating to the emergence of a truly pluralist world order. Religious scholars and faith leaders are contributing to this process by delving deep into their religious traditions to find out the foundations for peaceful co-existence and also making comparative studies of various traditions, through a meaningful dialogue among religions, in order to prepare the followers of various religions for a lot of give and take necessary for the adjustments within a pluralist dispensation.

India has always been a pluralist society. From times immemorial, various races, civilizations, cultures and faiths have lived here and prospered side by side, enjoying their spaces with complete freedom. The Indian experience of tolerance and co-existence, that is strictly rooted in her ethos, has no parallel anywhere in the world. The uniqueness of this experience lies in the fact that all the major world religions have not only found here a ground to sow their seeds and grow but also a cultural ethos of acceptance where it was possible for them to contribute to the flowering of a composite culture based on the synthesis of the best of all the religious traditions. It is this synthesis that we witness today expressing itself through poetry and philosophy, fine arts and architecture.

A thorough and penetrating study of Islamic culture and history reveals that Islam, too, believes in pluralism, though there is no reference to the term pluralism as we understand it today. The Qur'an and the Hadith literature abound in emphasis on tolerance and peaceful co-existence. Historically, various Islamic societies have, from the very beginning, been pluralist in nature where people of diverse races, colours, cultures and faiths have lived in peace and harmony. The Islamic jurisprudence and religious laws evolved through the centuries also reflect and recognize pluralism and inclusivism as a living reality. Islam has always showed an attitude of openness and acceptance towards different faiths and cultures. Muslims have generally treated their non-Muslim citizens with tolerance and fairness. There are many well-documented instances in Islamic history of Muslims, most notably the religious scholars denouncing in strongest possible terms and raising their voice against any excesses and injustice done to any non-Muslim by a Muslim commoner or elite in utter disregard to Islamic teachings. In what follows an effort will be made to bring out in some detail, on the basis of core Islamic sources, what the Qur'an and the Prophet of Islam (PBUH) enjoin to prepare Muslims to live in a pluralist society.

Why this world is peopled by such a diversity has a unique explanation in the Qur'an which says:

> "If thy Lord had so willed, he could have made humankind one people, but they will not cease to differ." (11:118)

The above quoted verse explains the divine scheme of human diversity and multiplicity of social and cultural identities. To support and strengthen this plurality, God Almighty enjoins that 'there is no compulsion in religion' (2.256). The Qur'an has expressed itself strongly against any forceful imposition of one's faith on others, and this admonition is directed to no less than the Prophet (PBUH) a person himself. The holy Book says:

> "If it had been thy Lord's wish, everyone in the world would have believed; will you then compel people, against their will, to believe." (10-99)

There is yet another instance where the Prophet (PBUH) has been asked to announce:

> "For you, your religion, and for me, mine." (109:6)

The Quranic injunctions clearly bring out the Islamic position that Islam not only does not have any room for any form of forced uniformity of faith but is also actively against it, and forbids it. Likewise, the verse 109:6 provides the guidance that Islam not only accepts other religions but also posits their peaceful co-existence. At another place the Qur'an says:

> "O people of the Book! Come to common terms as between us and you: That we worship none but God, that we associate no partners with Him; that we appoint not, from among ourselves, Lords and patrons other than God." (3:64)

Here the addressees are the People of the Book present at that time. These verses could be assumed to have addressed the people of other religions as well, offering to come together to talk on common terms.

Islamic view on the genesis and spread of mankind emphasizes the essential oneness of man:

> "O mankind! We created you from a single (pair) of a male and a female, and made you into nations and tribes, so that you may know each other. Verily the most honoured of you in the sight of God is one who is the most righteous of you." (49:13)

The Prophet (PBUH) has been reported to have said in a Hadith that 'All mankind is God's family.'

The God of Islam does not belong to Muslims alone but is the Creator and Provider of all mankind, even those who don't believe. And the Prophet of Islam (PBUH) has been described by God Almighty as a 'Mercy on all the worlds.'

Islam makes it incumbent on all the believers that they must have faith in all the previous prophets, without which their faith in Islam cannot be complete. Muslims also believe that God has sent His messengers and guidance to all the peoples in all ages (Qur'an 24:35). It is also an article of faith for the Muslims that all the Prophets have brought the same divine message and guidance. It amply shows that Islam accepts the spiritual continuity of human history and does not segregate.

When the Prophet of Islam (PBUH) migrated to Madina from Makkah, his place of birth, where he was about to be killed by his adversaries, he had to share space with the Christians, Jews and other non-Muslims who were an integral part of the Madinan society. It was a time when the first Islamic fraternity was being established and the Prophet (PBUH) recognized the presence of these non-Muslims faiths and concluded a treaty with them which has been recorded in Islamic history as the Treaty of Madina. This Treaty contains the principles that may still serve as a basis for founding a pluralist society. The Prophet (PBUH) recognized the Christians and Jews as equal parts of the Madinan society and gave them equal rights as citizens and full religious freedom. The Prophet never led any campaign against his adversaries at Makkah. All the battles he and the Muslims were forced to fight were fought outside Madina. After the fall of Makkah, the Prophet of Islam (PBUH) re-entered it, not as a conqueror but, as an ordinary man of God, with the least bloodshed and no reprisals. He forgave all those who had tormented him and made no attempt to forcibly bring them into the fold of Islam.

This policy of tolerance and peaceful co-existence even outlived the Prophet (PBUH) and caliphs and other Muslim rulers generally continued to make it a salient feature of the Islamic socio-cultural and political ethos. When Syria and Egypt fell to the Muslims, the Christian population of these places were accorded full religious freedom. No churches were demolished or converted into mosques. They were allowed to conduct their affairs according to their laws. They enjoyed the freedom to even eat pork and consume alcohol, the two things strictly prohibited throughout the world of Islam.

The second Righteous Caliph Umar offered a written assurance to the residents of Jerusalem when it fell to the Muslims: It is an assurance from the leader of the faithful and servant of God to the people of Jerusalem that they enjoy full protection of their life, property, churches and crosses and of other things related to their religion. Their churches would not be converted into dwelling places, nor would they be demolished, and there would be no coercion in matters of faith.

Non-Muslims living in the Islamic state were allowed to have, preserve, maintain and build new places of worship. Even the expenses on their upkeep and repairs were provided for from the state exchequer. Jewish rabbis and Christian priests were paid salaries and unemployed non-Muslims paid allowances from the state exchequer. During the caliphate of the third Righteous Caliph Uthman, the Bishop of Mero wrote to the Patriarch of Persia that the Arabs whom God has bestowed the domination of the world don't assail the Christian faith; on the contrary, they help our faith, treat our religious leaders and our monasteries with honour and provide grants to our Churches.

Non-Muslims enjoyed certain rights in the Islamic state that were denied to Muslims. They were free to trade involving interest which is prohibited for Muslims. In the event of external aggression, they were exempted from conscription. Religion never became an impediment in seeking employment in the Islamic state. Amir Muaviyah's finance minister and physician were Christians. During both the Umayyad and Abbasid periods, non-Muslims were appointed to high state positions. In the early Abbasid period, the department of medicine was almost totally manned by the Christians. Bait-ul-Hikmah, the great Academy of Wisdom founded by the Abbasid Caliph Mamoon-al-Rasheed had many non-Muslim intellectuals and translators. Christian and Jewish men of learning and translators had a prominent share in the Muslim efforts to bring Greek philosophy and science into Arabic that proved to be an essential inspiration behind the European renaissance. In Muslim Spain, being a non-Muslim was in no way a liability in terms of enjoying opportunities. The rights of non-Muslims were not only protected but also well guarded. During the Abbasid period, the governor of Egypt, Ali bin Suleman, ordered some Churches to be demolished. Musa bin Isa, who replaced him as governor had consultations with the *ulema* on this act of aggression. Lais bin Saad who was the most prominent among the *ulema* in Egypt denounced the demolitions and asked the governor to have them rebuilt at the state expense. The governor dutifully acted on the advice.

Islamic jurists and law-makers have always been alert and sensitive to the issues related to the non-Muslims and took care in incorporating provisions for them while compiling Islamic laws. *'Kitab-al Khairaj'* compiled by Imam Abu Yusuf, one of the most revered Islamic jurists, the most notable disciple of the great Imam Abu Haneefa and Chief Justice of the Abbasid Caliphate, contains principles and legal provisions to ensure the rights to be enjoyed by the non-Muslims in the Islamic state and to make them impervious to any infringements from the state authority.

An outline of Islamic position and Muslim orientation towards religious pluralism, which amply shows that Muslims have by and large expressed themselves and behaved in favour of religious inclusivism. There have of course been instances of serious breaches of rights and misconduct towards non-Muslims by certain rulers in India and elsewhere. But these are no more than mere aberrations and deviations from the strict Islamic position. It is so even today when a miniscule section of militant Muslims does not and is not allowed to represent the larger and extended Muslim community the world over. Militancy and extremism are anathema to Islam which characterizes the Muslims as being the 'people of the Middle Path'. Thankfully the dominant majority amongst the Muslims still believes and practices peaceful co-existence. That's why there is a growing urge and willingness within the Muslim community to reach out to their non-Muslim brethren and make serious efforts to understand them and let them have a deeper understanding of the Muslims, through a process of continuous interaction and dialogue at every level. We have to realize that to defeat the forces of exclusivism and hatred each and everyone of us who believes in the oneness of man and peace and harmony must contribute to this grand task of religious reconciliation which must at all costs have to be made a success, if we wish to make our country and the entire world a place for human beings to live and prosper.

11

Islamic Model for Social Harmony

Islam is the most misunderstood religion in the contemporary world. Thanks to the thoughtless adventures of self-styled crusaders trying to enforce at gunpoint their mistaken notions about religion, particularly Islam, it has got an image of an intolerant faith incapable of coexistence in plural societies. It is an image totally at variance with the tenets of Holy Qur'an and the preaching and practice of the Prophet (PBUH) which indeed provide a model for social harmony and hatred-free respectful coexistence among people of different faiths and cultures.

What needs to be kept in mind is that, like every new religion, Islam had appeared in an entirely non-Islamic milieu. It was able to grow and flourish not with the power of sword but because of superior moral conduct of its adherents. Its framework of social conduct can well be taken as a model for a civil society free from conflicts and committed to expansion of human knowledge and welfare.

The word Islam is derived from the root *Silm* which means peace and complete surrender to the will of the Creator. It is on this essential core of peace that the Quranic idea of coexistence is based.

Consider, for instance, the commandments about variety in modes of worship. The Qur'an enjoins:

> "Say, you that reject faith, I worship not that which you worship, nor will you worship that which I worship. And I

will not worship that which you have been wont to worship. Nor will you worship that which I worship. To you your way to me mine." (109:1-6)

Here is another injunction:

"Let there be no compulsion in religion. Truth stands out clear from error. He who rejects evil and believes in God has grasped the strong branch (of grace) which can not break. Remember God hears and knows all things." (2.256)

This attitude reflects the Islamic belief that as Allah is one His creation, the entire humankind, should not be treated as irreconcilably divided on the basis of variety of faiths. According to the Qur'an "all mankind is a single community (*Ummah*)."

The variety that we see is attributed to the will of God:

"If God had so willed, He could have made them a single people. But he admits whom He wills to His grace; and for the wrong doers there will be no protector nor helper."(42:8)

The idea is made more explicit in another verse:

"Men, we have created you from a male and a female, and made you into nations and tribes that you might get to know one another. The noblest of you in Allah's sight is one who is most righteous of you. Allah is wise and All-Knowing." (49:13)

In other words, if you have trust in Allah's wisdom and omniscience which you must have as a follower of Islam, you must understand that you are required to develop an understanding with and about others rather than having disputes and quarrels with them. God's grace can be attained by noble and righteous conduct and not by mere verbal adherence to Islam.

The Qur'an ordains belief not only in any one Prophet but in all His messengers who must be shown equal respect; meaning thereby that no distinction can be made between them. Only some of them, not all, are mentioned by name so that all who claim to have received revelation are worthy of respect. It is made more explicit in the Quranic verse which reads:

> "There are those who disbelieve in Allah and His messengers and seek to differentiate between Allah and His messengers and say: 'We believe in some and disbelieve in others and seek to choose a way in between the two such are disbelievers in truth and for disbelievers we have prepared a humiliating chastisement. But those who believe in Allah and His messengers and do not differentiate that between them, them Allah will certainly give their reward; And Allah is All-Forgiving, All-compassionate." (4:150,151,152)

Thus we see that respect for all Prophets, and the messages they have conveyed in the form of different religions, is a fundamental tenet of Islam. Those who show disrespect to any other religion, as did the Taliban of Afghanistan, in vandalising the Buddha statue, are guilty of violating the faith and the sin of disbelief. There is absolutely no place for hatred and injustice. The Qur'an commands:

> "O ye who believe! Be steadfast for Allah in equity and let not hatred of any people seduce you that you deal not justly. Deal justly that is nearer to your duty." (5:8)

> Believers ! Be upright bearers of witness for Allah, and do not let the enmity of any people move you to deviate from justice. Act justly, that is nearer to God-feaing.

So the essence of all religions (*Adyan)* being the same it is highly imprudent to quarrel over methods prescribed for practice of faiths.

The great Persian Sufi poet Jalaluddin Rumi has expressed this truth in the following words:

> "I have picked the essence from the Qur'an and thrown the bones to the dogs to quarrel over."

True faith in Islam requires not just being good and righteous towards other Muslims; it is also judged by the way you treat others. According to a tradition of the Prophet (PBUH), a true Muslim is one who does no mischief to any other Muslim but "the true Momin (man of faith who is superior to a formal Muslim in merit) is one who does no mischief to his neighbours and of whom they have no fear."

Obviously neighbour in this context stands not for a Muslim alone, but for non-Muslims as well.

God's command to the Prophet, according to the Qur'an, is:

> "Say (O Muhammad): O Mankind! I am the messenger of Allah to you all, the messenger of Him to whom belongeth the sovereignty of the heavens and the earth. (7:158)

and further: "We sent thee not save as a mercy for the people." (21:107)

It must be noted here that the Prophet (PBUH) is being called a mercy for all mankind, and not for Muslims alone.

With the Prophet being a mercy for all mankind and the Quranic tenet of peace leading to co-existence and tolerance, justice becomes the cornerstone of all individual and public conduct in an Islamic society. The concept of justice in Islam encompasses the recognition and protection of the rights of non-Muslim citizens of an Islamic State.

The Prophet (PBUH) was so concerned about the rights of the non-Muslims that he exhorted the Muslims:

> "Beware! On the day of judgment I will stand in appeal against any one who commits excesses against any *dhimmi* (the people protected under agreement) or cuts short his

rights or burdens him more than his endurance or receives anything from him without his consent." (Abu Dawood—*Kitab-al-Jihad*)

The Righteous Caliphs showed great sensitivity on this score. During the time of the first Righteous Caliph, Abu Bakr a non-Muslim woman who had abused Muslims had got her teeth broken as punishment by an officer. When it came to the notice of the Caliph he wrote to the officer concerned, Mahajir bin Umayyah:

"I have come to know that you have got two of the upper teeth of the woman, who sang derogatory verses against Muslims, broken. A warning could be sufficient had she been a Muslim and the punishment in this case should be even less than a reprimand. Being a *dhimmi* her singing these verses is nothing when her sin as great as the *shirk* (associating other gods with Allah) is being tolerated. Had I been able to warn you earlier you must have tasted the punishment for your excess.

The second Caliph, Umar made a will from his death bed:

"I make this will for the Caliph succeeding me that he must honour the agreement reached with the people whom the Prophet of Allah (PBUH) took under his protection, defend them and ensure that they are not burdened beyond their endurance."

The fourth Caliph, Ali stressed the same principle saying: "Do not reject any kind of peace and pact of co-existence to which your enemy invites you and in which there is Allah's satisfaction... If you conclude an agreement with your enemy or undertake an obligation, be faithful to your pact and carry out your commitments in full honesty and make your life a guarantee for the protection of your obligation.

The Prophet concluded many agreements with various non-Muslim groups in Madina. The agreement reached between the Prophet and the Christians of Sinai reads.

> "This is a writ according to which a treaty is concluded with them and whoever opposes its articles will be considered a transgressor to him (the Prophet) and other Muslims. Such a person will be rejecting Allah's promise...Whenever monks or travellers get together, and reside in the mountains or in the deserts, in inhabited places or in planes, in synagogues or in temples, we will be behind them to protect them, and I will defend their lives, property and goods with my life and that of my friends, helpers and nation, since they are my subjects and united allies."
>
> "With the exception of what they willingly pay as tribute, they will by no means be compelled to pay anything more or held responsible for it."
>
> "Their judges, monks, hermits and traveller's will not be molested, and no synagogues or churches will be destroyed and nothing of their property may enter the Muslims' dwellings." (Ibn Hisham's *Sirah*, Vol. 2)

With such explicit teachings of the Qur'an and the Prophet stressing the Islamic stance of non-imposition of religion and freedom of faith, Islam can in no way be perceived as monopolising the Truth. The peaceful co-existence of various faiths based on the Quranic vision of oneness of man being one of the articles of faith in Islam closes all likelihood of the sort of fanaticism that the Taliban and other forces of Islamic revivalism tend to equate with Islam. They are but signs of aberrations. Islam must not be reached through what Muslims do. To understand and experience real Islam, one must refer to its original sources, the Qur'an and the Prophet. And they are there to unite, not to divide the mankind.

12

Social Justice and Gender Equality

Justice is the opposite of tyranny. Tyranny is invitation to disorder and destruction while justice and equity open the avenues for positive progress. Justice and equity constitute the foundation of entire life. The stronger this foundation of a society, the better would be the condition of its members' life. Every crack in this foundation brings misfortune and trouble.

The Holy Qur'an, the foundational message of Islam attaches highest importance to justice and equity. So sensitive is Islam to these values that, in application of these values it ignores even the distinction of friend and foe. The Qur'an expressly declares this principle in the following words:

> "O believers! God demands of you to stand firm on Truth. Stand up to uphold Truth and Justice. Do not allow enmity with a community to deviate you from the path of justice. Do justice because it is the closest to piety."

The concept of justice is closely linked with equality among humankind. People of different colours, speaking different languages inhabit the earth. There is among them a variety of faiths and cultures. Some are prosperous while others wallow in poverty. If discrimination of high and low, superior and inferior be observed on the basis of these differences, it would be difficult for most people to have access to justice. Those of low status would stand deprived of equal opportunities and facilities in different walks of life. Thus an unending process of cruelty and injustice will start. Islam has, in this context, unambiguously proclaimed its viewpoint that all human beings are equal, being the progeny of the same Adam who had been born on earth. Thus the Qur'an says:

> "We have given respect and dignity to the entire progeny of Adam."

And, the last messenger of God declared:

> An Arab is not superior to a non-Arab (Persian or Ajami), nor is a Persian (Ajami) superior to an Arab. Similarly, a White is not superior to a Black and a Black to a White. Superiority depends entirely on piety."

The spirit of social justice runs throughout the teachings of Islam. For example, the road to progress, education and knowledge, is open to all. Nobody has a monopoly over knowledge; there is no priestly class, whoever wants can get knowledge and attain highest stature in the field of learning. The guide and teacher of humanity, the Prophet, has declared:

> "Acquire knowledge. The acquisition of knowledge is the duty of every Mussalman." History of Islam is witness that people of poor descent-even servants and slaves-rose to such high status in learning that even princes and kings became their disciples. Avenues of trade, economy and legitimate professions are open for all. Islam awarded a share to the poor in the wealth so that the gulf between the rich and the poor does not get too wide and all human beings should be able to fulfill their needs.

> Islam assures to everybody security of respectful life, freedom of thought and action, equality before law and security against punishment till the offence is proved. There is a famous incident during the times of the Prophet. A lady of a respected family, accused of theft, was brought before the Prophet with recommendation to forgive her. The Prophet responded firmly

saying, "If my daughter Fatima had committed theft, I would have punished her too." (*Bukhari*, 3965)

There are numerous instances of social justice in the life and lofty teachings of the Prophet. The covenant entered into at Mecca is a landmark in respect of providing help to the oppressed and making secure the rights of the weak. This socially significant step taken together with people of other faiths was so dear to the Prophet when he said, "I will come if I am invited for this cause even after I cease to be Prophet. (*Seerat, Ibn-e-Kaseer*, 07/1).

An equally shining example is the Madina Covenant which was meant to unite a multi-religious society on the basis of religious and social freedom as a measure of security against outside threat. It is wroth following in the contemporary multi-religious society, in particular, and in every age in general.

The best Charter of Justice is found in the last address Jum'tul-Wida; it articulated for the first time the ideas of human equality, human dignity, human rights and human values. It was a beautiful cascade that reflected an ideal combination of thought and action.

Gender equality is an important part of social justice. Gender discrimination and oppression of the weaker sex have been an integral part of human history. There have been many ups and downs in the search for a solution of this problem. On these pre-Revelation efforts, Iqbal had written:

> Hazaar baar hakeemon ne isko suljhaya
> Magar yeh mas'la-e zan raha waheen ka waheen

(A thousand efforts were made by the wise to solve the problem But the problem of women remained unmoved, unsolved.)

And it was so despite the fact—

> Wujood-e-zan se hai tasweer-e-kainat mein rang
> Isi ke Saaz se hai zindagi ka soz-e-duroon

(Life has its significance because of the female kind. It provides the music for the inmost feelings of humanity.)

The Revelation solved this problem by giving a clear and unambiguous concept a thousand years ago. While proclaiming honour and dignity of mankind it accorded equal respect to the entire progeny of Adam. As such there is no distinction of gender in regard to human dignity in the eyes of Islam. Both man and woman are equal and have equal status. Both are equal before law; the value of the blood of a woman is the same as that of a man; the murderer of a woman will be punished the same way as the murderer of a man.

Prayer and nearness to the Creator is the need as well as the religious duty of everybody. Piety and fear of God could be the quality of a man or a woman both will get the same status and love of the Almighty. The Qur'an says:

> "Whosoever, man or woman, is pious in conduct and has faith, will surely be granted better life."

The Qur'anic verse *Ahzaab* makes parallel mention of both man and woman eleven times which is a clear indication of the equality of gender in respect of all qualities and prayers. Woman is in no way dependent on man in respect of prayer, fasting, performance of *Hajj* and offering *zakaat* or in observing other religious duties. She can attain the highest status on the basis of her piety and purity. The names of Hazrat Rabia Basaria and Hazrat Syeda Nafisa are written in golden letters in history on account of their prayers and abstinence in the path of God. Islam has not only provided equality of opportunity for acquisition of knowledge but also made it equally a duty of both.

In this context it should be clearly understood that Islam does not make a distinction between worldly knowledge and religious learning because the material objects are as much the gift of God as faith. Faith, in fact is nothing but the conduct of life in accordance with the will of God. Of course Islam makes a distinction between good and evil deeds; knowledge that is useful for the one who acquires it as well as for humanity at large is good. Seen in this perspective, the importance to learning given by Islam becomes evident. That is how one third of the knowledge that the Prophet bestowed on mankind in the form of Shariat and law and through the agency of his companions came through a woman. The community received one third of the Shariat through the agency of Syeda Yesha Siddiqah; highly placed companions used to visit her for this knowledge and Muslims came to know of the details of the family life of the Prophet from her.

The encouragement of learning, at the hands of the Begams of Bhopal, is a proof of the same concept of gender equality. The share of women in the field of politics becomes evident from the time when the Prophet ordered his companions to make the sacrifice and open their robes (ahraam) and none came forward to obey the order on account of the deprivation from off-season pilgrimage (*Umra*), the Prophet turned to Hazrat Umm and she told him to go out and perform that function. After that the companions also followed him. In the early wars between the believers and non-believers, women used to take part along with men and treated the wounded and provided drinking water to soldiers. Syeda Zainab, a scion of the family of the Prophet is an outstanding example of political struggle.

Rights of women is an important part of the concept of gender equality. Islam has been highly generous and broadminded in this respect. The rights that Islam has conferred on women are not seen anywhere else. Rights to learning and prayer have already been mentioned, so has equality of the value of life.

In this context, it is worth taking note that in today's civilized world also attempts are made to get rid of the female child even before birth. In the pre-Islamic age of ignorance, the Arabs used to bury the female child alive. Note the description of the evil practice given by Islam:

> "When any of them is given the news of the birth of a girl child, his face darkens and he feels so humiliated that he shuns company of other men, contemplating whether he should keep the ignominy or bury it in earth." Don't we

see the same picture today! The Holy Qur'an took strong note of this practice, declared it evil and illegitimate and warned that whoever commits this horrible crime will have to answer for it before God. The verse *Takveer* reads:

"When the girl buried alive will be asked." (81:8)

The Prophet also told that one who brings up two girls to adulthood, will be as close to God as are two fingers of a hand. (*Muslim*, Hadith 4765)

Economic rights are an important item in human rights and Islam has accorded several economic rights to women. In terms of financial rights the woman holds a permanent position, according to Islam. She does not get lost in the personality of her husband. Therefore, if she continues her business even after marriage or if she has some other income she has exclusive proprietary rights over all her assets. The Prophet's wife Khadija owned a flourishing business and she had even helped him from her finances. It is because of independent in financial position that woman has been given separate duty for *zakaat*. Whatever gifts the woman receives from her parents or relatives are her property.

Another noteworthy financial right is the right to inheritance. She gets a share from the property of her parents as well as her husband. And this right she can get at any stage of her life, whether a child, adult, married or unmarried, divorcee or widow. Whenever the legatee—father, mother, brother, sister or husband—passes away, she has a claim on their property as laid down by *Shariat*. And, this share comprises of property, land, business as well as cash.

Financial right also includes the responsibility of her maintenance on the father before marriage and on the husband after marriage. Islam has not put the burden of her maintenance on the woman. On the contrary, Islam has ordained that the husband should pay her a suitable amount as *mehr*.

In respect of marriage, matrimonial rites and divorce also women have been given specific rights. According to Islamic

Shariath, matrimonial rites cannot be performed without the consent of the woman. She can marry according to her own choice although in this regard she can consult other members of her family for advice. Islam has honoured women by making marriage a firm contract. But if living together becomes impossible they can separate; while the man enjoys the right to divorce, woman can exercise the right to dissolution of marriage.

In sum, every page of Islam carries significant mention of the gender equality. Equal rights, in fact in some respects, additional rights are given to a woman. Once a companion asked the Prophet, "Who is the most deserving of my good conduct?" The Prophet replied, "Your Mother!" Then he was asked, "Who after that?" The question, having been repeated thrice received the same response, while asked the fourth time the Prophet's reply was, "Your father." (*Muslim*, 4622) This *hadith* shows that mother's stature is thrice higher than the father's.

If the woman is a daughter, her education and upbringing is the message of heaven. As a good wife she is the most precious wealth. (Muslim, 2668). If she is the mother her feet are the place of paradise. (*Nasai* Sharif, 3053)

This place of woman shows the concept of gender equality in Islam.

Before I conclude I would like to explain why men have been described as the syrup of women and they have been placed a notch above women. (Nissa' 34, Buqra 228) It means that home is an institution and man has been nominated its head so that he is responsible for all expenses for running the institution. His higher position only indicates this responsibility. In all other spheres of life the rights of woman have been already described in terms of the Qur'an and *Hadith*. Keeping these details in mind let us turn to this tradition of the Prophet were he says:

Tirmazi says: (Arabic—Tirmazi) or "Woman is part of man.". The Qur'an puts the same idea in its inimitable style thus: (Arabic—Al-Imran 195) "You are part of one another. And, further:

> "They are your garments and you are theirs", (*Al-Baqarah*-187).

13

Islamic Education for the Development of Nation's Welfare

Bridging the Gap Between Developed and Developing Countries

Islam is basically a knowledge-centric religion. Knowledge in its myriad manifestations, from the consciousness of God and self to the efforts to know about the natural world, has been emphasized in the holy Qur'an and by the Prophet of Islam, to the extent that without knowledge it is very difficult for one to become a Muslim, for, becoming a Muslim is always based on a conscious choice made by an individual. The holy Qur'an repeatedly calls for thinking and meditating on things around, the natural phenomena as well as the happenings in the inner world, and drawing conclusions about the existence of God as the Creator and Sustainer of life and the world. Islam in this sense is a thinking religion that provokes human beings to keep their sense perceptions alive to the signs of the divine presence, use their power of reasoning that has been bestowed on them by God to wonder at the marvels of the creation and try to comprehend that all these perfectly symmetrical and systematic phenomena of nature could not have come into existence without a creator who is omniscient, omni-present, all-knowing and all-pervading.

The centrality of knowledge in Islam is marked by the fact that the very first revelation that the Prophet received was about knowledge. It said 'Read in the name of your Lord who created...

.' (6:1) In sura Al-Baqara, the holy Qur'an relates the story of how knowledge originated. The story thus goes in the words of God:

> When your Lord said to the angels: I am about to place on earth a vicegerent. They said: Will you place on it one who will spread mischief and shed blood, while we celebrate Your glory and extol Your holiness. He said; 'Surely I know what you do not know.' Then he taught Adam the names of all things and presented them to the angels, and said: 'Tell Me the names of these, if what you say be true.'
>
> 'Glory to you', they replied, we have no knowledge except what you taught us. You alone are wise, knowing', Then said He to Adam: 'Tell them the names of these things.' And when Adam had told them the names of all things, He said; Did I not tell you that I know the secrets of the heaven and the earth, and all that you reveal and all that you hide? (2:31-33)

The Quranic story establishes the essential fact that the origin of man and the origin of knowledge, according to the Islamic vision are equal. It emphasizes that man is not essentially a sinner but was endowed with the knowledge of things and his fall from heaven was not because of any elemental depravity but due to Adam's momentary disregard for the God-given knowledge.

Another Quranic *Surah,* Al-Rahman, opens with these verses, 'He has taught the Qur'an. He created man and taught him articulate speech.' (55:1-4)

Omniscient and All-Knowing are the attributes of God that find prime importance in Islam. The Islamic concept of divinity has the knowing as its essential component. Knowledge is light and ignorance is darkness. Allah sends His messengers with the light of knowledge contained in His Books to the people. The holy Qur'an says, 'We have revealed this book so that, by the will of their Lord, you may lead men from darkness to light'. (14:1, 2)

This Islamic vision of knowledge is naturally linked to

the propagation and dissemination of knowledge, which is further consolidated by the fact that the Prophet of Islam has been repeatedly described as a teacher, educator and communicator, who has been sent to the people to teach them the Book and wisdom. The Prophet, in one of the Traditions, says 'I have been sent as a teacher (Ibn Maja: 225). And the Prophet's entire life, all his words and deeds, bear testimony to the radiant fact that both as a human being and as a Prophet, he was always a teacher, not in a narrow formalistic sense but in its broadest connotation. He not only exemplified the significance of knowledge in human life and society, but also made elaborate arrangements to institutionalize the idea of knowledge and its propagation. Moving even further, the Prophet accorded a sanctity to knowledge. He emphasized that 'seeking knowledge is a duty' (*Ibn Majah:220*) and further strengthened this effort by saying that 'The one who steps out in the way of knowledge remains in the way of God, till he returns' (*Tirmidhi*: 2571). He again glorifies this search for knowledge by saying that 'God makes way to heaven easier for the one who makes endeavours to seek knowledge' (*Tirmidhi*: 2570).

Even a cursory look at the Prophet's life is sufficient to prove that he passed each and every moment of his Prophetic mission in teaching, educating and communicating the divine wisdom and practical day-to-day knowledge. He was always thronged by the people with queries about everything under the sun and problems of all sorts, and he sent them all back fully satisfied, unburdened and enlightened. He spoke to all, both men and women, with a day fixed exclusively for women, at their own demand. The Prophet encouraged his companions to learn different languages. Zaid bin Thabit, thus, learned Syriac language. The paramount importance the Prophet gave to education was again evident when after the Battle of Badr he decided that the prisoners of war who knew to read and write could find freedom by teaching the Muslim children to read and write.

Universalization of education was another pioneering initiative that the Prophet of Islam took to make knowledge available to all human beings irrespective of race, class, creed, colour, gender or social status. Contrary to the exclusivisation of knowledge and the practice of confining its seeking only to the upper castes or classes, the Prophet ensured that each and every Muslim not only received knowledge but also passed it on to those who were deprived of it. He sent his companions to far-off places to impart knowledge and spread education. He impressed upon his companions that they must share with others what they learn from the Prophet. It was women who benefited the most from this universalisation of knowledge. By bringing to women the right opportunities to seek knowledge Islam generated an educational movement that was unimaginable for the world at the time of the Prophet, as it was a world where almost in all societies women were considered inferior to men and deprived of all rights to exist as independent human beings. By throwing open the doors of knowledge to women, Islam took lead in their emancipation and empowerment and made them equal to men in all worldly and religious matters.

So, inspired by the teachings of the holy Qur'an and the Prophet, the Muslims took upon themselves the duty of seeing to it that seeking of knowledge and promotion of education was thoroughly institutionalized. During the entire Islamic history we see a firmly established system of education taking roots and great centers of learning coming up throughout the length and breadth of the Islamic world. Almost all men of religion, right from the earliest great compilers of *Hadith* down to the great imams of *fiqh*. Interpreters of the Qur'an and philosophers also acted as teachers and educationists and contributed to the institutionalization of education. *Kuttabs* or *Maktabs* were a necessary presence in all Muslim societies and served as the basic centres of education where the holy Qur'an and elementary religious subjects were taught.

Bookshops and booksellers have always enjoyed a very important place in Muslim societies. In the Baghdad of Abbasid period, markets were full of books available on the pavements and libraries flooded with thousands of books. Documentary evidences like Ibn-al Nadim's *Al-Fihrist* and Yaqut's *Mujam al-Buldan* and *Mujam al-Udaba* amply show the flourishing business that the booksellers had enjoyed in those times.

Private collections of books and houses of the learned men also served as sources of inspiration for the promotion of knowledge. These houses were the centres of knowledge as well as repositories of cultural values and cultural goods. It has been vividly recorded in history books that the great philosopher and man of medicine Ibn Sina, while being immersed in his philosophical meditations and medical research, always found time for the promotion of learning. He used to sit in his house to read from *al-Shifa* and *al-Qanun* to a large number of people. Likewise Abu Sulaiman al Sijistani Muhammad bin Tahir bin Bahram was a leper and one-eyed, so he ceased to appear in public. But his hosue drew lots of students and scholars in search of knowledge and inspiration. Al-Ghazali, after wandering far and wide in search of true knowledge for about eleven years, finally settled at Tus to teach theology and Islamic spiritualism at his home.

Ameer Ali in his celebrated book 'The spirit of Islam (London, 1922, pp. 361) elaborates a *Hadith* in the following words:

> The Prophet preached the value of knowledge because one who acquires it in the way of the Lord, performs an act of piety; who speaks of it, praises the Lord; who seeks it, adores God; who dispenses instruction in it, bestows alms; and who imparts it to its fitting objects, performs an act of devotion to God. Knowledge enables its professors to distinguish what is forbidden from what is not; it lights the way to heaven, it is our friend in the desert, our society in solitude, our companion when bereft of friends; it guides us to happiness; it sustains us in misery; it is our ornament in the company of friends; it serves as an armour against

> our enemies; with knowledge, the servant of God rises to the heights of goodness and to a noble position, associates with sovereigns in this world, and attains the perfection of happiness in the next.

This tradition of the Prophet of Islam lays down the essential characteristics of knowledge and the qualities it engenders in a human individual. Seeking of knowledge, according to the Prophet, can be an act of worship and piety if carried out in the way of God; it makes an individual conscious of what one should do and what one should desist from; it serves as a companion; it gives power of personality and self-realization that act as armours against enemies; it raises a common individual to the heights of being a sovereign in this world, and finally it is an investment for attaining the state of bliss in the Hereafter. The Prophetic Tradition presents a holistic concept of man that true Islamic knowledge brings to actualization. This view of man combines body and soul, matter and spirit and this phenomenal world and the permanence of the Hereafter into one single whole of human existence that becomes meaningful only by bringing to life through one's actions God's scheme of things on this earth. The poet-philosopher Iqbal in his famous *Lectures on the Reconstruction of Religious Thought in Islam* has elaborated this point by saying:

> The ultimate reality, according to Qur'an, is spiritual and its life consist in its temporal activity. The spirit finds its opportunity in the natural, the material and the secular. All that is secular is, therefore, sacred in the roots of its being. The greatest service that modern thought has rendered to Islam and, as a matter of fact, to all religions, consists in its criticism of what we call material or natural—a criticism which discloses that the material has no substance unless we discover it rooted in the spiritual. There is no such thing as a profane world. All this

immensity of matter constitutes a scope for the self-realization of the spirit. As the Prophet so beautifully puts it: 'The whole of this earth is a mosque.'

This idea of man and knowledge provides us the Islamic perspective on how the human affairs can be conducted in a way that satisfies both the material and spiritual demands of life in a holistic manner. In other words, this is the basis of what we term today as sustainable development as the most humanly beneficial view and way of material and moral growth.

The world we live in today is marked by intense inequalities and inequities between the developed and the underdeveloped parts of the world on one hand and between those who enjoy all the fruits of progress and those who are deprived of everything and have been thrown to the periphery of the process of development, on the other. This is a world where all the material resources and wealth have been monopolized by a powerful few who seek to control them to keep the rest of the world and human beings in utter servitude and penury. This is a world where knowledge and access to it and its production and distribution have become the sole preserve of a few nations in the world and the knowledge-elites within nations. It is an extremely pathetic and perverse situation where knowledge, which ideally should be an emancipator and democratiser, has been turned into a source of enslavement, bondage, and exploitation.

It was in the seventeenth century when Europe, energized by the Enlightenment, woke up to the secrets of the natural world which it started unraveling to initiate a process of scientific discoveries and inventions unprecedented in human history. Knowledge was now recognized as a source of power much more than the one of self-realization and moral and spiritual ascendancy. The powers that science and technology put in the hands of western man were exploited to generate a materialistic momentum that led to the initiation of the Industrial Revolution. This Revolution, for the first time in human history, saw man subdued and over powered by machine, a human creation, and all the moral and spiritual values trampled upon by the forces of unbounded greed and exploitation. The ominous outcome of this all was the establishment of the capitalist economic order together with the rise of the process of colonisation of Asia, Africa and Latin America at the political level and colonization of mind at the intellectual plane. The rest of the story is now part of history that still keeps unfolding in the form of bloody confrontations between the mighty and the weak.

There is UNO and a legion of other international fora where the idea of a just and equitable world order remains under discussion in flowery and mystified language, often by those who themselves are the cause of most of the injustice and inequity in the world, while the poor and the underdogs, both nations and people, go on crying themselves hoarse on the streets outside.

What then is the remedy? Is there a remedy at all? How can the realities be married to ideals and the blood of ideals infused into the anaemic veins of realities? This again brings us back to the fundamental questions relating to the nature of knowledge, the concept of man and the ways about internalizing knowledge and its dissemination. All change in the phenomenal world is but the reflection of the changes within. This has been one of the basic tenets of all religions, much against what Marxism teaches. As Iqbal has said:

> It is fresh ideas that fresh worlds spring forth from
> For mere stones and bricks cannot create a human world.

The reflective and meditative content of human consciousness, the ideas and concepts and above all, the civilizational matrix and spiritual fecundity of man have always been the breeding grounds of new realms of human creativity.

Of all great religions of the world, Islam has offered clear guidance, as discussed above, for man to become truthful and just and work to create a just and equitable society and world order. Islam lays down three cardinal principles that serve as corner-stones for creating a God-oriented human individual and society that in turn become basis for a just world order. These principles are:

1. Khilafah (Vice-gerency)
2. Amanah (Trusteeship)
3. Adalah (Justice)

The holy Qur'an puts man on the high pedestal of being the Khalifah or vice-gerent of God on earth. Man has been created in God's image and endowed with all the mental and spiritual powers and material resources to carry out this mission assigned to him by his Creator. According to the Qur'an, the entire universe and everything under the sun have been made subservient to man and he is free to use all these resources at will. But here a rider has been added that he is not free to use them to destroy them, which brings us to the second principle of Amanah.

As vice-gerent of God, man holds all the powers and resources bestowed upon him by divine mercy as a Trust and he has to use them accordingly. Man is duty-bound to make an equitable and just utilization of these powers and resources for the welfare of all.

Justice is naturally the logical corollary of the two foregoing attributes as without justice the actualization of the Khilafah and Amanah is impossible. The holy Qur'an places highest emphasis on justice and calls it 'nearest to piety' and equates its absence with darkness. Justice is also the central attribute that attracts other Islamic attributes of tolerance, equality, universal brotherhood and co-existence.

The world today has its cup full of woes and miseries. With all its predicaments and crises, made even more intractable by its intransigence to recognize their seriousness, our world seems to be clueless about a way out. All talk of development and progress boils down to material prosperity which the mighty few do not wish to share with the deprived millions. The materialistic concept of development has been shown to be inadequate because divorced from all moral and spiritual values, it can no more bear the burden of its contradictions. So it is tottering and will soon collapse, unless strong remedial measures are taken by those who hold a holistic concept of man as an article of faith.

An Islamic intervention, based on the above-mentioned Islamic principles is, therefore, the need of the hour, to bring about a paradigm shift in the development strategy of the world. But it is always easier said than done. The question is who will take the initiative and from where? Muslim nations and societies, as we see and have them today, seem to be the least capable of making a difference as most of them are themselves engulfed by the same materialistic rush of things and concepts. Indeed, there are many enlightened and perceptive individuals and organizations, which, with their right Islamic perspectives and conduct, can take up the challenge. But the task of effecting a paradigm shift in the world development strategy, both at intellectual and practical planes, is too daunting to be within the capabilities of a few individuals or organizations. All the intellectual, moral and spiritual resources of entire nations need to be marshaled to arrive at a point from where a new beginning can be made. And more importantly, before we do it, we will have to put our own house in order, only to bear witness that we practise what we preach. Islam first needs to be rehabilitated in its traditional dwelling places before it finds new habitation in human hearts and minds, to usher a new era of true equality, equity, justice and emancipation.

14

Significance of Muslim Media in the Context of Misinformation on Islam

The significance of the media vis-à-vis Islam reflects serious realization of a grave challenge that the Muslim community all over the world faces, especially in the context of revolutionary changes in information technology and globalization of the 21st century.

The challenge has not been presented only now in the 21st century. It has been there since the time of the Crusades when European powers, ambitious to reverse the advance of Islam, with its civilizing role, had made fast inroads into that continent when it was acting as carrier of human wisdom. Thanks to the teachings of the Prophet (PBUH) who imparted to the Arab Muslims not only the values of human equality, mutual cooperation, humanism but also the importance 'to gather wisdom from wherever it was available'; the Muslim leadership of the first few centuries after receiving the message, gathered knowledge from all corners of the world. The achievement of the period was not only the Cordova mosque but also the tremendously rich library they set up in Spain thereby unleashing the process that culminated in the Renaissance and Reformation. Jawaharlal Nehru has paid fulsome tributes to that role of Arab Muslims in recognizing that if Islam had come to India via Arabs it would have fostered in its people a spirit of scientific thinking.

Unfortunately, the success of that period developed in the leadership of that time un-Islamic tendencies of self-indulgence, self-glorification and territorial covetousness contrary the teachings of the Prophet, who had enjoined austerity, humility, and refusal to temptation to possess what belonged to others, ignoring the developments in knowledge and human consciousness. The result was that they failed to keep pace with the development of new techniques even of warfare which their rivals mastered. It was then that started the onslaught on Islam; Muslims began to be accused, through all media, oral and written, as fanatical, tyrannical, murderous and rapacious. The challenge needed to be met at that time but the community failed to understand it, complacent with memories of their past glory and satisfied with the luxuries they were enjoying. The Moghals, for example, willfully neglected the use of printing press and continued to enjoy the beauties of calligraphy.

It is the accumulated burden of these lost centuries that muslims have to carry today. Even if they resolve to face the challenge today it is not too late, though late. *(Der Ayad Durust Ayad)*. Yet it is important to measure the magnitude of the challenge as well as its source so that an appropriate strategy to meet it may be evolved. In that lies the significance of Muslim media; it does not exist and needs to be evolved. Had a Muslim media existed we would not have been discussing, as we are, the role of media in different Islamic countries.

The fact that the world outside Indonesia does not know the developments in theory and practice of Islam that have been made in Indonesia is a manifest proof of the absence of such an entity as Muslim media. Similarly, if anti-Islam media is talking about clash of civilizations our media should have, but has not, adequately projected the idea of dialogue among civilizations propounded by President Khatami. So is the case with the views about Mahathir Mohammad's opinion expressed in the recent OIC conference. Abdurrahman Wahid's interpretation of Islam has remained confined to his native land and some academic circles even though it has won appreciation of the committee that decides the Megsaysay Award.

Media battle cannot be fought by living in one's own narrow world; it requires entry into the open field. The world does not talk of a Christian media or a Zionist media because both are alive and kicking and claim to be the mainstream media of the world while catering to the anti-Islam prejudices. Why should the media projecting Islamic viewpoint not be a part of the mainstream media particularly when the message of Islam is not for Muslims only but for entire humanity?

What is meant by Muslim media today? It is the media controlled by Muslims in various countries, not one that presents the realities and facts of contemporary life in terms of the teachings of Islam. It is Muslim because it is promoted, owned and patronized by Muslims in their respective countries, no matter whether it serves the needs of the community or of humanity at large as understood by Islam. The most glaring fault of the Muslim community in this respect is that it has failed to develop its media in the language that has become the linguafranca. The Christian media has attained universal acceptability because it has moved beyond Latin to more modern English, French and German. The Zionist media leads the mainstream opinion because it is no longer stuck with Hebrew and put all its energies and resources in capturing the minds of English-knowing segment of the humanity which today determines the trend of knowledge and thinking of the world. We have confined ourselves to the local languages in Islamic countries and the minority language like Urdu in India. And, the Truth of Islam is still confined to Arabic and, to some extent Persian.

Muslims have to ask themselves how many non-Muslims understand or appreciate their view of Islam as presented in these media? Why only non-Muslims, even among Muslims it has become a monopoly largely of the section whose perceptions are not based on empirical reality but suffer from the complex of living in a hostile world. The answer is there in the situation we are facing because not only is the language a barrier but the presentation also remains esoteric and turgid which alienates and repels rather than attracting non-Muslims. On the other hand, the so-called modernist Muslims either echo the hostile western viewpoint or try to fit Islam in a terminology borrowed from the hostile West. 'Fundamentalist', for example, was an expression originally used for Christian fanatics opposed to any interpretation of the text of Bible, even to its translation from original Latin into any modern language but we have unhesitatingly, without reservation, adopted it when the Western powers used it to condemn the Iranian Revolution against monarchy. Even when offering a defence of Islam, we only say we are not fundamentalist without caring to ask what is wrong with adhering to fundamentals if they are in tune with the realities of life.

These observations are based on the Indian experience where Muslims are facing a difficult situation, along with the rest of the world Muslim community, as large sections of people are being bombarded by Western media motivated by forces out to conquer and subjugate the globe for their selfish gains. And, there is no worth while effort to counter the propaganda. The number of newspapers owned and/or edited by Muslims runs in thousands and, in that sense, India can be said to have a Muslim media but it is non-existent in the sense that its impact is not felt. It must be able to influence Muslim as well as non-Muslim media persons to understand the Muslim situation in the context of world situation. That would be possible if only the facts are presented to prove that the onslaught on Islam or Muslims is a threat to not only Muslims but to the entire human society. That means Muslim media has to be sensitive to the problems faced by other sections of humanity; the problems faced by Muslims and Muslim states are shared by most of the developing nations and weaker sections in each nation.

It is the case not specific only to India, the Muslim world has not been able to develop a viable media because powerful sections of the Muslim world, with the exception of Indonesia, Malaysia, Iran and India have failed to develop a democratic temper. Media flourishes in a democratic environment. Islam is perceived by the world in the light of its performance in West Asia where pilgrim centres and institutions exist which are revered by the Muslims all over the world. Had the ruling establishments built their own nations in the image of the teachings of Islam based equality, fraternity and justice, the values that constitute a democratic picture of Islam in the world would not have been the one projected by inimical forces. Had they used their natural wealth to promote the causes of the nations that attained independence after the recession of imperialism in the post-World War period, anti-Islam propaganda would not have succeeded in influencing large sections of population there.

The reasons for this state of affairs have been enumerated in a recent publication, *Media aur Mussalman* by Arshad Amanullah, as follows:

1. Absence of objectivity;
2. Introvert character;
3. Inadequate professionalism;
4. Lack of resources, financial and technological;
5. Limited narrow readership circle;
6. Dependence on Western news agencies;
7. Over-dependence on Urdu language;
8. Near exclusive dependence on print media.

How can this situation be remedied? A few suggestions as a consumer, and only as a practitioner of the art are presented here for careful consideration:

First, a mass media training school of international standard be set up to train young Muslims to enter the field of journalism so that they may join different newspapers and news-agencies. There are eminent Muslim journalists who have acquired a place of respect in the non-Muslim media; their help can be taken for such a venture. Jamia Millia Islamia has taken an initiative in this direction with its Institute of Mass Communication which turns out trained hands for electronic media. It needs however to be investigated why it has not produced desired effect on media. Besides, it does not have facilities for training newspaper journalists in different Indian languages, especially English. Competent trainees from among Muslims would come to such an institution only if they find job opportunities which in the present conditions are almost non-existent, there being scarcity of media wedded to human good and has become an increasingly profit-oriented industry.

Secondly major Muslim newspapers and journals in India are published in Urdu; they should be a model of objective journalism, fair and humane. Islam's insistence on Truth makes it incumbent to maintain objectivity so that Muslim masses develop an adequate and balanced understanding of contemporary reality along with Islamic consciousness. Objective presentation will make them attractive to Urdu-knowing non-Muslims as well; thus creating an all-round atmosphere of respect and appreciation for their viewpoint. They should avoid being too closely identified with any political party or religious sect and should have a broader appeal. Unfortunately, the Urdu press has fallen a prey to the prevalent tendency to sensationalise through overemphasis on the woes of Muslims, hardly ever pointing out how it affects the moral and material well being of the society as a whole. They give an impression of a community suffering from inferiority complex whereas Islam is meant to make its adherents more confident.

Muslim media ill-serves the values of Islam. As against the profit-oriented Urdu media we have the missionary media which projects a sectarian view point of different Muslim organizations competing to win the allegiance of the community without bothering in what colours their stand shows Islam to the world beyond their narrow circle. Besides, there should be adequate recognition of the media that projects the problems faced by Muslims sympathetically in true perspective. The role of media in the context of Gujarat (2002) and Iraq War should be duly appreciated. So should be the role of Muslim and non-Muslim journalists in what is known as the non-Muslim or mainstream media.

Third, seminars and workshops be organized to make the educated section of the community aware of the character and role of media. These gatherings should not remain vacuous intellectual exercises and must come out with practical suggestions to improve the situation. The primary task they have to keep in mind is to develop a common understanding of the problems faced by the community across sects and parties and infuse the need for collective action.

Fourth, steps be taken to bring about proper changes in ownership pattern of Muslim media so that the resource constraint can be overcome. It may be a Trust or a Limited company financed by Muslim industrialists as well as enlightened prosperous Muslims in other countries. Who can promote this and how? Unless a guiding force in this direction is created a change in the ownership pattern is difficult. A conference like this one, convened with the cooperation of an international organization can goad the community towards this end.

Fifth, the successful Muslim newspapers be persuaded to start editions from different cities by using Internet and satellite services. That will also induce them not only to broaden their perspective but also introduce comprehensiveness and variety to attract a broad spectrum of readership.

Sixth, there is the need to make use of recent technological developments. For some reasons, subjective and objective, Muslims have not been able to project Islam in its true perspective through film and TV media. Special efforts should be made to sponsor attractive programmes to present the true picture. Same is the case with computer technology.

Last, though not the least, there urgent need is an to develop democratic temperament. Media, it must be understood, flourishes in a democratic milieu.

Recently I came across a well-researched book *Maghribi Media aur Uske Asaaat* by Nazrul Hafeez Nadvi. It has attempted to expose what it terms as the conspiracy to impose global

(American-Jewish) culture on the entire human society. The author at the end leaves the reader with the impression that the attempts of the West are inevitably self-defeating. It may be reassuring to the Muslim community that the truth of their faith is so-self-evident that by just proclaiming it the onslaught on Islam would be defeated. This can lead to a sense of complacence which has been one of the weaknesses of the community. Muslim media, to be effective, must remain on guard in respect of these temptations.

This is an example of the absence of a democratic temper which recognizes the people merit's only if they accept your viewpoint whereas the democratic spirit demands an acknowledgement of merit even in those who hold a different ideology. That in fact is also the message of the Qur'an that has emphasized that it is calling humanity to the message that has been sent through various prophets in different regions of the world. It also enjoins that we should not only own our own blemishes but also must repent and provide recompense for it. It will not serve the purpose of making Islam the voice and conscience of humanity unless essential humanity in others is duly recognized and the blemishes within are owned.

I have started on this somewhat critical note not because I am bitten by the self-flagellation bug but because I am conscious of the role of Islam as a reformer-saviour of humanity. Lack of its guidance will be a tremendous loss to not only the community but to the humanity at large because it is facing the challenge of globalization which is making covetousness and competition to possess more and more wealth even at the cost of moral values.

In the late 19th and early 20th century, when European imperialism was at its zenith and the continents of Asia, Africa and Latin America seemed to be helpless, Muslim leaderships in Turkey, Egypt and India had given lead in combating the scourge; they share the credit for rolling back imperialism. In India Sir Sayyad initiated the process of realizing the importance of scientific thinking and acquiring modern knowledge and Maulana Azad exhorted the Muslim community not to remain aloof from the national struggle for freedom because, if it is the patriotic duty of Hindu majority it is the religious obligation of the Muslim community. It has to be noted that their impact was felt largely due to their competent use of the media.

It is therefore necessary to create a media that should be able to effectively communicate to the world the true picture of the community and the truth about Islam. Not only should this media be able to educate Muslims about the true meaning and significance of Islam and help it to be in step with the march of times without losing their bearing, but also impress the other media and other communities with the need to understand Islam as the message concerned with establishing equality and peace among different segments of humanity.

15

Islamic Teachings

Maternal Health and Adolescent Reproductive Health Issues

India is a vast country. Its population increased from 36 crores in 1951 to 102.7 crores in 2001. This rapid growth is often seen as uncontrolled explosion and is considered as one of the key factors holding up India's progress. It has to be understood that the population growth occurs naturally and has taken place in all regions of the world. In the earlier days, when public awareness and education were not so popular the birth and death rates in the population were very high; with the advances in public health, as happened in our country quite considerably since independence, the death rate has started to decline rapidly, while the birth rate still continues to rise, and this has led to the condition of rapid growth of the Indian population.

Despite the fact that the couples now prefer fewer children than before, the overall growth in numbers still continues to be higher because of population momentum.

The number of young persons in India is very large. Even if the couples continue to prefer having smaller families of one or two children, for some more time to come, the birth rate is likely to go up because of the large number of young couples.

The overall burden of reproductive ill health is very high and many women die every year due to the complications of pregnancy and child birth. Maternal mortality may persist for a while which points to the inequity in women's access to the basic life saving intervention as well as certain inadequacy of the health care system. Most maternal morbidity and mortality occur due to hemorrhage, sepsis, toxemia, obstructed labour and unsafe abortion, while safe and affordable technologies do exist. Equally important issues related to this are nutritional anaemia, adolescent pregnancies and gender discrimination. The problem of neonatal health and morbidity and mortality is a matter of grave concern.

India's National Population Policy's main concern is about economic and social development. It looks for improving the quality of lives of its people, enhance their well being and to provide them with the opportunities and choices to become productive assets in society.

Human development is basically concerned with the well being of people, as the 'people' are the most valuable resources of any country. The reproductive health profile of India is a matter of major concern.

In India women marry early and soon after menarche. The average age at which the women in our country commence menarche is 13.5 years and mean age at marriage for female adolescents is 14.7 years. Notionally the main age of marriage is almost similar for rural and urban areas with difference of about one year.

In most cases of early marriages, the justification for early marriages stems from the firm conviction that it would prevent a girl from possible promiscuity, and this belief is rampant cutting across caste and class boundaries.

Maternal health though, at present, improved considerably, it still continues to be compromised. There are various reasons which can be attributed to this phenomenon;

- Early marriage
- Poor antenatal care
- Poverty leading to lack of proper diet
- Unsafe sexual practices

- Contract of STDs or other infection
- Lack of health care facilities, particularly in the country side
- Abortion:
  - Low level of awareness about MTPs
  - Unsafe abortion practices
  - Sex selective abortion etc.
- Lack of proper post natal care
- Improper child care, including lack of immunization facilities etc.
- Misconception about family planning in certain sections of society.

ADOLESCENT REPRODUCTIVE HEALTH

As far as adolescents are concerned, the present scenario in India reflects poor knowledge levels on issues of reproductive health. Only a small percentage of adolescents have the correct information about sex, and sexual and reproductive health issues, which is known to lead to unhygienic and harmful practices. Inadequate access to reproductive health care continues to be a major problem among the youth.

One out of every seven persons in India is an adolescent. It is known that the behavioural pattern during adolescence often lasts a life time.

The consistently high rate of adolescent childbearing in India is an issue of concern to policy makers because of the serious negative social, economic, and health consequences associated with it. Despite an increase in the number of health facilities, antenatal care during pregnancy is not widespread. One out of three female adolescents do not receive antenatal care.

During the past few years, the issue of adolescent pregnancy has been increasingly perceived as a social problem. The International Conference on Population and Development (ICPD 1994) identified adolescents as a distinct target group in need of *ad hoc* reproductive health programmes and services.

In India, adolescent motherhood is closely associated with early marriage leading to early initiation of sexual activity. In Indian society, early motherhood as well as large family size is still considered ideal to ensure that an optimum number of children especially sons are there, to provide old age security for parents.

Adolescents, therefore, who comprise more than ¼th of population need to be focused on.

- They should be properly educated and helped to get knowledge, values and skills for making informed choices in life, particularly in relation to sexual behaviour.
- They should be properly educated not to indulge in unsafe sexual practices and to adopt healthy reproductive life style.
- Growing problems of female foeticide should be immediately challenged and for this the following steps should be considered:
  - Programmes should be designed to educate people about the importance of girl child, gender equality and hazards of unsafe abortion.
  - Unintended pregnancies should be taken care of
- Sex with other than the legitimate partner as well as premarital sex should be avoided which is also the best way to challenge HIV/AIDS and other STDs.
- Mothers, before and after delivery, should be given special attention.
- Females in the society should be given equal rights and husband-wife communication on certain important issues of life should be improved.
- The literacy rate among the population should be improved
- Statutory laws, e.g., MTP Act 1972, and Prenatal Diagnostic Techniques, Regulation and Prevention of Misuse Act (1994) need to be strictly enforced.

- Males should be properly made to understand about the equal rights of females.

In India, human well being is the core concern of development and population stabilization. But discrimination against women is still widespread, rooted in the social system where women are less valued than men.

Of course women have many significant socio-economic attainments to their credit. These changes do not really indicate any fundamental gender biased mindsets and in the lower social position of women.

The Ministry of Health and Family Welfare, Govt. of India, in consultation with certain other organizations, has been taking important steps in addressing and tackling these deep rooted problems.

The Govt. of India has designed several programmes which are concerned with the:

- Improvement of socio-economic status of the people.
- Developing responsible sexual and reproductive behaviour among adolescents.
- Controlling and spreading awareness about unsafe sexual practices.
- Restricting single partners for sex.
- Avoiding unnatural sex.

It is also true that, these measures are receiving considerably good response within society. The reproductive and child health interventions that are being implemented by the Govt. of India, are expected to provide services and achieve multiple objectives. There has been a positive paradigm shift from method mix target based activity to client centered demand driven quality services. The Govt. of India is making efforts to reorient the programmes and change the attitudes of the service providers at the grass root levels as well as strengthen the services at the outreach level.

- Antenatal care and immunization services
- Contraceptive prevalence
- Family planning
- Awareness about STD's/HIV/AIDS, etc.
- Utilization of govt. health services, etc.

ISLAMIC TEACHINGS ON MATERNAL AND ADOLESCENT REPRODUCTIVE HEALTH

The Qur'an, the Shari'ah, and teachings of Prophet Muhammad (SAWS) also speak volumes about sex, sexual behaviour of humans and reproductive health etc. Islam gives special attention to these core issues.

Studied deeply, Islam has answers to almost every problem being encountered today with regard to sex, and maternal and reproductive health.

Though, certain parts of the world are following these practices, other countries like India have yet to fall in line in true spirit so as to achieve maximum benefit.

Islamic teachings have an answer, may it be to almost all the problems mentioned about the adolescents, maternal health and related issues

- Concept of marriage
- Education or literacy
- Foeticide
- Unsafe sexual practices
- Unnatural sexual behaviour
- Gender equality
- Premarital or extramarital relationship
- Care of mother and child
- Status and rights of a female, etc.

The Government has also taken up issues like education, literacy, foeticide and gender equality, to get a more balanced and optimum benefit. If these Islamic teachings are adopted in true spirit, the ideal condition in the society could be achieved.

Marriage

Islam recognizes the strong sexual urge and desire for reproduction as natural. Islam encourages marriage as a legal sexual means and as a shield from immorality (sex without commitment).

Prophet Muhammad (PBUH) says, "Marriage is my tradition, he who rejects my tradition is not of me." (*Bukhari, Muslim*)

"Marriage is half of religion, the other half is being God, fearing. (*Tabrani*)

Gender Equality

Unlike the general belief that Islam is very chauvinistic and oppressive towards woman, Allah treats men and women as spiritually equal (Qur'an 3: 195):

> "I never fail to reward any worker among you for any work you do, be you male or female, you are equal to one another... ."

The spiritual equality between men and women is reiterated in 4: 124 as follows:

> "As for those who lead a righteous life, male or female, while believing, they enter paradise, without the slightest injustice" and again in 16:97:

> "Whoever does good and believes—Whether he is male or female. Such shall enter the Paradise and they shall not be wronged"

> "Anyone who works righteousness male or female while believing, we will surely grant them a happy life in this world, and we will surely pay them their full recompense for their righteous works."

Sex Education in Islam

The Qur'an has placed great emphasis on acquiring knowledge, and in the days of the Prophet (PBUH), Muslim men and women were never shy to ask questions including those related to private affairs such as sexual life.

Sex is an important aspect of our life. Allah in the Qur'an has discussed reproduction, creation, family life, menstruation and even ejaculation. Prophet (PBUH) who was sent to this world as an example has also discussed sexual and reproductive life at various times. At the time of Prophet (PBUH), sex education was imparted along with other teachings of Islam.

Islam recognizes the power of sexual need and this subject is discussed in great detail in the Qur'an and the sayings of Prophet (PBUH) in a serious manner. Parents in India should familiarize themselves with this body of Islamic knowledge.

Prophet Muhammad (PBUH) says, "When one of you have sex with your wife, it is rewarded as an act of charity." The companions surprised and said, "but we do it purely out of our desire, how can it be counted as charity". The Prophet (PBUH) replied "if you have done it with a forbidden woman, it would have been counted as a sin, but if you have done it in legitimacy, it is counted as charity."

Sex Outside Marriage

About adultery Allah says in the Qur'an, "Do not go near to adultery, surely it is a shameful deed and evil opening roads (to other evils)" (17: 32)

"Women impure are for men impure, and men impure are for women impure, and women of purity are for men of purity and men of purity are for women of purity (24: 26).

Prophet Mohammad (PBUH) has said in many places that adultery is one of three major sins.

Islam forbids all types of sexual relations outside marriage, premarital or extramarital. Islam advocates a number of specific measures to temptations that may lure one into such relationships.

1. The Prophet encouraged all followers (especially the youth) to get married so that their natural desires are legitimately fulfilled.
2. Polygamy is allowed by Islam in a bid to reduce the number of unmarried women in society.
3. There are clear instructions to women to cover themselves and to appear in a modest way so as not to attract men.
4. Boys are not allowed to associate with girls after puberty.
5. Alcohol consumption, parties, dancing involving both sexes—practice and setting which can lead to sexual relations outside marriage are forbidden.
6. Meetings between a man and a woman where they are without other company is forbidden.

WOMEN'S STATUS AND AUTONOMY IN THE ISLAMIC CULTURAL CONTEXT

A husband and wife form the nucleus of a family. Their relationship is described in the Qur'an as having two major qualities; love (passion, friendship, companionship), and mercy (understanding, reconciliation, tolerance, forgiveness).

Abortion

The main concern for theologians is whether the Shari'ah is supportive of abortion or not. From this general question, certain sub questions arise:

- At what stage during the term of pregnancy does the foetus become a human being?

- What are the circumstances in which Islamic law permits abortion and under what circumstances is abortion prohibited?

In the interpretation of the Qur'an and Hadith, direct reference is made to the ensoulment of the foetus 120 days after fertilization. There is a consensus among Muslim scholars that abortion is not allowed after 120 days. However Islam gives women the right to abort in cases of severe maternal problems. However, these rights are relative and should still be weighed against various alternatives.

Right to Contraception

The right to use contraceptives is discussed by many Islamic scholars in detail. Most of the scholars are of the opinion that non-permanent methods of contraception are allowed in Islam provided that they are safe and they are accepted both by husband and wife. However, the question of permanent methods (male and female sterilization;) still requires clarification. Most of the scholars are of the opinion that these methods are not permitted except in cases where the health of the mother is in danger.

Sex During Menstruation

Islam forbids sex during menstruation.

Anal Intercourse

The Prophet (PBUH) says, "Verily Allah is not ashamed of truth. Don't approach women via their backs (anal intercourse) (*Al-Bukhari*)

As narrated by Abu Hurairah (RATU), the Prophet (PBUH) said: "Cursed is he who goes to his wife by her back." (*Al-Bukhari*)

Islam gives women and men the right to sexual health by forbidding all that is believed to be harmful. In addition, it provides them the right to sex education and enjoyment. However these rights are not to be practiced outside legal marriage.

Within the framework of Islamic teachings, reproductive health implies the ability of men to live from birth to death with reproductive choice, dignity and to live free of reproductive health diseases and risks. In addition, the ability of a married couple to enjoy marital sex without fear of infection, unwanted pregnancy, or coercion, to regulate fertility without risk of unpleasant or dangerous side effects; to go safely through pregnancy and childbirth and to bear and to raise healthy children.

16

Islam, Universality, Physical Health and Wholesomeness of Life

Islam is not merely an abstract metaphysical idea of God or a philosophy distant and removed from life or a call to renunciation and withdrawal from the world or an ideology to be discussed and debated and made a basis for waging wars. Islam is just about how men should live and conduct themselves in this world and about his relations with the universe and other fellow human beings.

Islam is a way of life, an attitude to life, faith in human values and the principles of conduct to which a person should subscribe in all sincerity and which he should translate into practice before he may call himself a Muslim and can be so regarded by others. It further makes the claim that it embodies the message, which other great prophets proposed and preached. And this message, which has been a continuity through the ages, is that of peace and universal co-existence.

The word 'Islam' is derived from the root 'silm' which means peace and complete submission to the will of God. The word Muhammadanism, as is often used for Islam, is a misnomer and misleading, for the Prophet of Islam never ascribed the religion to himself. To him it was a religion which he was inspired to preach, the basic idea of which is peace—peace to all mankind. The usual greeting amongst the Muslims is, 'Assalam-o-Alaikum'—peace be upon you, whoever are you, also reinforces this emphasis on peace.

The faith in the oneness of God, as is fundamental to Islam, also means faith in the oneness of mankind because the God of Islam speaks to all mankind—the children of Adam. The Qur'an says:

> "Verily We have honoured the children of Adam. We carry them on the land and the sea and have made provision of good things for them and have preferred them above many of those whom We created with a marked preferment" (17:70)

A tradition of the Prophet emphasizes the same theme:

> "The whole mankind is God's family. He holds him the dearest who does the most good to His family".

The universal man that Islam has envisaged is marked by his ability to do justice with all (*al-Nas,* i.e., all mankind) and not merely his co-religionists. Under no circumstances is unfairness to anyone, even the worst enemy, justified for according to the Qur'an, "all mankind is a single *ummah* or community (2.213) and the differences that divide them are there, so that they may be recognized (49:13). The Qur'an stresses that one should do good (*Ihsan,* i.e., beneficence, kindness) not only to one's parents and relations but also the orphans, the needy, the helpless, and the neighbours whether they are related to one in any way or not at all (17:24—26). This Quranic command is reinforced by a tradition of the Prophet, which says:

> "A true Muslim is one who does no mischief to any other Muslim", but "the true Momin (man of perfect faith who is superior to a formal Muslim in merit) is the one who does no mischief to his neighbours" and "of whom they have no fear". Here no distinction is made between a Muslim and a non-Muslim; all his neighbours should be satisfied that there is not even a likelihood of any evil coming from him.

The Qur'an is so much concerned with justice and fair play

that it enjoins the Muslims not to deal unjustly even with their proclaimed enemies. It says:

> "Do not let your wrath against the people who have barred you from the Holy Mosque move you to commit undue transgressions, rather, help one another in acts of righteousness and piety, and do not help one another in sin and transgression"
>
> "And let not your hatred of a folk who (once) stopped your going to the inviolable place of worship seduce you to transgress, but help ye one another unto righteousness and pious duty. Help not one another unto sin and transgression".(5:2)

Whenever the Qur'an speaks of fellow human beings (An-nas) and the importance of dealing with them justly and kindly, it does not enunciate the principle with reference to Muslims only but to all mankind, whatever their religious beliefs or social standing, with whom they may have any dealings. It insists that honesty and fairness are called for in all matters, great or small, from everyday transactions from buying and selling to the national policies adopted in war and peace, whether the parties concerned are Muslims or non-Muslims. Nothing can be a greater travesty of Quranic truth than to imagine, or believe, that Muslims will not be called to account for any act of dishonesty or the breaking of faith or committing excesses against non-Muslims.

It was this attitude of compassion and forgiveness inspired by the stern sense of justice that prompted the Prophet to have mercy on those people of Mecca who had cruelly persecuted him and other Muslims. Some of his followers came to him once and requested that he invoke the wrath of God upon them. His quiet reply was: "I have not been sent to curse anyone but to be a source of *Rahmat* (beneficence) to all". There is yet another example of the great generosity and forgiveness that the Prophet was capable of. When he entered Mecca, his place of birth, as a victor from where he had been forced to migrate because of excessive persecution and threats of physical extermination, the Meccans were afraid that they might be punished for their misdeeds. But all that the Prophet did was that entering Mecca, seated on a camel, he was heard reciting the following verse from the Qur'an:

> "There is no censure from me today on you. May God who is greatest amongst forgivers forgive you".

He also announced that the army of Muslims was not to interfere with anyone who took refuge in the Kaaba, or anyone who took refuge with a local resident, Hashim bin Khuzan, or anyone who was wounded. It was not to kill any captive, not to follow anyone who was running away. It amounted to declaring a general amnesty for everyone. The same practice was followed by his successors. The first Righteous Caliph Abu Bakr, while sending his army to Syria gave the following instructions to his commander-in-chief:

> "You will find amongst them persons who have devoted themselves to worship and prayer. You are not to interfere with them in any way. I direct you to observe these injunctions. Do not kill any child, woman or old man. Do not cut any fruit trees. Do not lay waste any towns or villages. Do not kill any animal except goats and camels for food. Do not burn any garden or oasis. Do not show any dishonesty in the disposal of booty. Do not show any cowardice". The fourth Righteous Caliph Ali, who was also the Prophet's son-in-law laid down these rules in greater details for the guidance of his army. The rules are:
>
> 1. Never begin a war yourself. God does not like bloodshed. Fight only in self defence.
> 2. Never be first to attack your enemy. Only repulse his attacks but do it bravely.

3. When reciting the *Rajaz* (a poetic recital before actual fighting) do not waste your time and, instead of speaking about yourself and your deeds, speak about God and the holy Prophet.
4. Never follow and kill those who run away from the battle or an encounter. Life is dear to them; let them live as long as death permits them to do so.
5. Never kill the wounded who cannot defend themselves.
6. Never strip a dead man for his dress.
7. Never cut the nose or ears of the dead to humiliate them.
8. Never molest or outrage the modesty of a woman.
9. Never take to loot and arson.
10. Never hurt a woman even if she swears at you or hurts you.
11. Never hurt a child.
12. Never hurt an old or an enfeebled person.

It cannot be said that Islam does not envisage the possibility of use of force at all or does not stand up against those who go out of their way to deprive others of the right to follow Truth as they see it. It is certainly right to resist such encroachment of freedom but even while permitting the use of force to resist the evil, the Qur'an is always careful to point out that forgiveness is better. The Qur'an says:

> "Nor can good and evil be equal. Repel evil with good; then it will happen that he between whom and you was enmity will become your warm friend. And who will rise to this height (of goodness) except those who exercise patience and self-restraint and who have been given an ample share of goodness. (41:34,35)

The Qur'an calls upon all men to "cultivate in themselves the attributes of Allah". This implies that the compassion which God shows to His creatures must be mirrored in the personality of a Momin. It is a reflection of God in man. Not only in the Qur'an but also in the traditions of the Prophet is stressed again and again that, "If you love Allah, you must love all his creatures". This intimate relationship between love for God and love for one's fellow beings has been beautifully brought out in the form of a parable in a well-known *Hadith* of the Prophet:

> "On the day of judgment God will ask a man: O son of Adam, I had fallen ill and you never attended me. Surprised, he will ask: How could that be possible? Thou art the Lord of the Universe. God will reply: Do you not remember that a neighbour of yours was ill and you never turned to him in solicitude? If you had gone to see him you would have found Me by his side. Then He will ask, O son of Adam, I asked you to give Me food but you refused! The man would reply: How could Thou be in need of anything? God will reply: Do you not remember that one of My servants asked you for it but you refused. If you had fed him, you would have found Me by his side. Then He will say: I asked you for water but you did not give it to Me. Again he will ask: How is it possible that Thou, the sustainer of the worlds, should be thirsty? God will again answer: A servant of Mine asked you for water but you did not give it to him. If you had done so, you would have found Me by his side".

The Qur'an depicts God as almighty but it also depicts Him both as beneficent and merciful. God's creation is a gift of God's grace. A *Hadith* says: When God completed the creation He wrote the following which is with Him above His throne, "My mercy has taken precedence over my anger".

In Islamic tradition both the sovereignty and beneficence of Allah are described as present realities, indicating that the creative power of God continues to be expressed in Allah's on going creation of the world. Allah is sustainer and guide of all life, in the present as well as the past. There is a sense in which it may be said that Allah continually recreates the world every moment or as the Qur'an puts it, "God originates creation, then repeats it. This aspect of Allah's creativity is given special emphasis when human birth is discussed; the foetal development of humans is attributed to the creative power of

Allah. The creation theology of Islam then, is not intended primarily to describe some primordial act of God's creativity but rather confess Allah's ongoing creative role in the present life of believers and their world.

Allah, the Qur'an says, created the world neither "in jest" nor "for naught", that is, God has a serious purpose for the creation. The purpose of creation is to serve Allah and to be submissive to God's will. This view of the creation implies that the creation's primary function is religious or devotional which means that Allah's creation is good and appropriately prompts a response of praise. Human beings are expected to respond to the honour Allah bestows on them with worship and gratitude. The status of vice-gerency bestowed on Man is a test to see if he obeys the will of Allah and acknowledges His sovereignty in an attitude of humility, repentance, loyalty and faith. Another purpose of creation is to provide signs of Allah's sovereignty and beneficence. These signs are intended less to provide an intellectual proof for the creative activity of God than to evoke gratitude in humans as they observe the wonders of creation.

Noteworthy is also the fact that this devotional purpose applies to the non-human creation too. "Whatever is in the heavens and in the earth—let it declare the praises and glory of God: for He is the exalted in might, wise". (57:1). "From the thunder to the angels, from the birds to the hills, all creation is to join in the praise of Allah" (13:14). It suggests that all of creation should be respected by humans as it also worships Allah. Islam values all life, not just human life. Animals are to be treated with compassion and concern, partly because they are God's creation, partly because they have a role to play in the devotional functions of all creation.

The Qur'an considers non-human living beings as communities. It says: "There is no animal on earth, nor a bird that flies with its two wings, but they are communities like your own" (6.38)

One may tend to believe that the status of vice-gerency

bestowed on man in Islam entails that man has been given the right to control all the creation and the environment to its will. But the Islamic emphasis on the sovereignty of God out-weights such consequences of the human vice-gerency which in essence means exercising care for the rest of creation, not violating or exploiting it wantonly.

Life in the Islamic world view is a trust that God has bestowed on man. It is a gift of God to man. It must be preserved and cultivated and lived in the service of God and fellow human beings, and not be wasted in vain. That is also why Islam forbids suicide as man does not own his life but is just a trustee of it.

Like life, the physical health is also a gift of God which should be protected from illness. There are many sayings of the prophet which stress the importance of health and treatment of illness.

A tradition says: "Healthiness and freedom (from stress, strain and hardship) are two of the most precious gifts of God. (*Dzad-at Ma'd*).

The Prophet has exhorted his followers to seek treatment of illness. He says: "God has not created any illness for which He has not created a medicine (*Bukhari, Muslim*). Another tradition has it: "Some Bedouins once asked the Prophet "O Messenger of God: If we do not seek treatment will it be a sin for us? The Prophet replied "Yes, O, slaves of God! You must seek treatment for yourselves. God has not created an ailment but for one that does not have remedy." They enquired "what is that ailment". The Prophet replied, "That is senility". (*Tirmidhi, Nasai, Ibn Majah*).

These categorical declarations that there is a remedy for every ailment and that to seek a treatment is not a sin proved to be very revolutionary at a time when diseases were considered all over the world to be signs of divine displeasure and the only remedy in popular perception was offering sacrifices to gods. This also proved to be a source of hope for patients. Moreover, it encouraged and inspired a process of research in medical science which the Muslim scientists raised to great heights.

Lastly a word on the Prophet's attitude towards leprosy and its victims. In an age when leprosy was taken as a sign of divine wrath and a scourge, and the leprosy patients were abandoned and secluded to fend for themselves the Prophet of Islam, according to a *Hadith*, took hold of the hand of a leprosy patient and made him eat from his bowl, saying: "eat in the name of Allah and have trust in Him" (*Tirmidhi*). This is only natural for a Prophet who, according to the Qur'an, has been sent as a mercy on all mankind. By this uncommon act of kindness he removed the horror and stigma attached to a leprosy patient, recognising him as a human being afflicted by a disease which can be cured.

17

Arab Islamic Civilisation

Past and Future—An Indian Perspective

Humanity today is living under the spell of globalisation. In this world might is right and material profit the king. Nations and individuals within nations are competing with one another to attain a dominant position in the fields of economy and political power. No value is attached to the ideals of sharing material gains and/or political power. Millions and billions of the poor and the underdeveloped are left to wallow in poverty, illiteracy and disease.

This globalised world is the consequence of the developments of science and technology that the West has developed and is now using to exploit and dominate the rest of the world. The irony of the situation is that the knowledge that has led to these dazzling developments is the gift of knowledge that the Arabs, inspired by the Prophet of Islam, bestowed upon Europe which was then in the grip of ignorance and superstition. And the beneficiaries of that gift are repaying the debt by accusing Islam as the source of fanaticism and terrorist violence.

Contemporary humanity, by and large, seems to have lost the memory of the great civilisational role played by Arabic speaking people. Inspired by the message of the Prophet (PBUH) they created an environment of peace based on the principles of freedom, equality, fraternity and social justice. It was an environment in which the Arab Muslims were able to hold sway over vast territories extending from the Atlantic in the West to the borders of China in the East. These territories came under the Muslims because they released them from tyrannical rulers, as also opened the avenues for knowledge.

The teachings of the Holy Qur'an and the precepts of Prophet Muhammad provided lofty ideals that created a civilization which paved the high road to enlightenment. It led to another kind of globalization directed towards welfare of the entire humanity. The Qur'an repeatedly urges Muslims to closely observe natural phenomena and to ponder over the mysteries of the universe and of the human psyche. 1t emphasizes the pursuit of knowledge as the key to all-round well-being and development. The Prophet (PBUH) regarded the acquisition of knowledge and learning as an obligation on every believer. He declared that "wisdom is (like) the lost animal of a Muslim; he should catch hold of it wherever he finds it." He exhorted his followers to carry the torch of knowledge and enlightenment far and wide, and warned against concealing or withholding it. Islam opened the portals of knowledge to one and all, men and women, rich and poor, king and slave. This refreshingly open, dynamic and egalitarian approach to knowledge brought about far-reaching and revolutionary consequences not only for Muslims but also for the human civilization as a whole.

After studying Amir Ali's 'History of Saracens' Gandhi had observed: "When the West was sunk in darkness a bright star rose in Eastern firmament and gave light and comfort to groaning world."

Between the fifth and fifteenth centuries, when Europe was enveloped in the Dark Ages, the Iberian peninsula under Muslim rule witnessed a spectacular efflorescence of science and medicine, philosophy and literature, technology and engineering, art and architecture and, above all, of tolerance and multiculturalism where Muslims, Christians and Jews lived and worked together in unimaginable harmony. Samuel ha-Nagid, a Jewish rabbi, was appointed the vizier of the kingdom of Cordoba. He led his largely Muslim soldiers into battle, with prayers on his lips for the victory of his beloved land.

Amartya Sen, in his recent books *Identity and Violence: The illusion of Destiny* (Penguin, 2006) and *The Argumentative Indian* (Penguin, 2005), has written that when Maimonides, the Jewish philosopher was forced to emigrate from an intolerant Europe in the 12th century, he found a tolerant refuge in the Arab world. His host, who gave him an honoured and influential position in his court in Cairo, was none other than Emperor Saladin.

Sen quotes a contemporary writer Maria Rosa Menocal who says in her recent book *The Ornament of the World: How Muslims, Jews and Christians Created a Culture of Tolerance.* (Little Brown, 2002) that by the 10th century, the achievement of Cordoba in Muslim-ruled Spain in being "as serious a contender as Baghdad, perhaps more so, for the title of the most civilized place on earth" was due to the constructive influence of the joint work of Caliph Abd al-Rahman III and his Jewish vizier Hasdai ibn Shaprut. Menocal argues that the position of Jews after the Muslim conquest "was in every respect an improvement, as they went from persecuted to a protected minority."

Even today, the Spanish tradition cannot be understood without the Islamic legacy and cultural heritage. Spanish language is replete with thousands of words of Arabic origin. Most of the family names as well as names of places and regions in Spain betray their Arabic origins. The regional division of Spain into 17 communities points to the continuing legacy of the Muslim period.

SOCIAL JUSTICE

According to the Islamic view, all human being have been created from a single primordial pair (Qur'an 49:13) and are therefore equal. In the Islamic view, the distinctions of birth, lineage, class, wealth or caste are inconsequential. The only worthwhile distinction or honour is piety and moral virtue. Thus the Qur'an says: "O mankind! We created you from a single (pair) of a male and a female, and made you into nations and tribes, so that you may know each other. Verily the most honoured amongst you in the sight of God is the one who is the most righteous of you" (Qur'an 49:13). In his sermon during the Last Pilgrimage, the Prophet (PBUH) declared: "O people! Verily your Lord is one and your father (Adam) was one. Verily an Arab is not superior to a non-Arab nor is a red-skinned person superior to a dark-skinned person, nor is a dark-skinned person superior to a red-skinned person, except in respect of piety and righteousness. All Muslims are brothers unto each other."

In Islamic society, social justice is institutionalized under the auspices of the state, an independent judiciary, and a comprehensive system of endowment *(Waqf)*. The Islamic state, especially through the state treasury *(Bayt at-mal)*, became a key instrument of social justice and public welfare. During the caliphate of Umar, the state treasury was greatly expanded and became a great source of sustenance and security for substantial numbers of poor and destitute people. The state treasury played a multiplicity of roles in Islamic society, including offering financial support to the needy, the disabled and the deprived sections of society, advancement of loans to the needy and the repayment of their debts, rehabilitation of victims of natural calamities, providing stipends to different categories of people, providing care and support to children who have no parents or relatives to take care of them, subsidies to peasants and cultivators to improve the means of cultivation, construction of canals, roads and bridges and the management of public hospitals.

In Islamic society, the judiciary is independent of the ruling dispensation. The judge *(Qadi)* is required to implement the provisions of Islamic law *(shariah)* without fear or favour and in the discharge of his obligations he is accountable, not to the powers that be, but only to God. An independent judiciary played a crucial role in ensuring compliance with Islamic law on the part of the ruling establishment as well as the general public.

An important dimension of social justice is gender justice. Islam has made a note worthy contribution to gender justice. Islam strictly prohibited the pagan practices of female infanticide and child sacrifice. The Prophet described the birth of female child as a sign of divine mercy and blessing. The honourable status of women in Islam is attested by a saying of the Prophet: "The world is an ephemeral thing, of which one takes temporary advantage, and among the things of the world nothing is better than a good, virtuous woman." He exhorted Muslims to be kind and considerate towards their wives. He declared: "The best amongst you is the one who is the most kind and considerate towards his wife." In an age when women's rights were virtually non-existent, Muslim women were given full rights to acquire, inherit and dispose of personal property without let or hindrance from relatives, including the husband.

ADVANCEMENT OF SCIENCE

George Sarton, the celebrated historian of science, has written:

> "The Muslim empire was created with the willing collaboration of Greeks, Persians, Copts, Christians and Jews. But this assistance does not wholly explain what might be called as the miracle of Arabic sciences, using the word miracle as a symbol of our inability to explain achievements which were almost incredible and unparalleled in the history of the world"

The Islamic contribution to science and medicine reached the zenith of its glory between the ninth and the thirteenth centuries. During this period, Europe was steeped in ignorance, barbarism and superstition. George Sarton has listed a galaxy of Muslim scientists from 750 to 1100 AD and again during the thirteenth century. The intellectual and scientific movement, which blossomed in the Islamic world, played a key role in ushering in the Renaissance in Europe. Robert Briffault perceptively remarked about the role of Arabs in stimulating the Renaissance:

"The Arabs kept alive the higher intellectual life and the study of science in a period when the Christian West was fighting desperately with barbarism. From the 12th century every one in the West who had any taste for science, some desire for light, turned to the East or to the Moorish West...When at the Renaissance the spirit of man was once again filled with the zeal for knowledge and stimulated by the spark of genius, if it was able to set promptly to work, to produce and to invent, it was because the Arabs had preserved and perfected various branches of knowledge, kept the spirit of research alive and eager, and maintained it pliant and ready for future discoveries"

GLOBALISATION OF SCIENCE

A movement for the globalization of science and philosophy was set in motion in the Islamic world during the medieval period. This movement was marked by extensive translations of scientific and philosophical works from Greece, India, Persia and Egypt, a synthesis of the researches of Muslim scientists and those of other lands, the establishment of scientific institutions, the employment of Arabic as the lingua franca of scientific research, translation and communication, and the creation of a community of scientists and translators from different religious, ethnic and regional backgrounds. Roger Bacon acknowledged that almost all of Aristotle's works were available only in Arabic translations, with only a small percentage having been translated into Latin. He asserted that without Arabic, Greek knowledge would have never reached the Europeans. Montgomery Watt has remarked that no people in the world translated from foreign languages as much as Muslims. George Sarton, has observed that, prior to the 15th century, almost all the works of classical writers were available only in Arabic. Bishop Alvares of Cordoba wrote in the 9th century:

> "All the young Christians, who distinguished themselves by their talent, know the language and literature of the Arabs, read and study passionately the Arab books, gather at great expense great libraries of these, and everywhere proclaim with a loud voice how admirable is that literature"

He acknowledged the debt of Arabs with the comment:

> "It is highly probable that but for the Arabs, modern European civilization would never have arisen at all. It is absolutely certain that but for them it would nor have assumed that character which has enabled it to transcend all previous phases of evolution, for although there is not a single aspect of European growth in which the decisive influence of Islamic culture is not traceable, nowhere it is so clear and momentous as in the genesis of that power which constitutes the paramount distinctive force of the modern world and the supreme source of its victory: natural science and the scientific spirit"

Paying glowing tributes to the magnificent contributions of Muslim astronomers and mathematicians, David A. King has observed:

> "The Muslims developed a mathematical theory for the effect of refraction at the horizon. They devised tables and instruments for solving all of the standard problems of spherical astronomy for any latitude. They developed the astrologic quadrant from the astrolabe. They prepared tables of coordinates for making curves on astrolabes and sundials and made substantial progress in instrumentation. They devised graphical representations of the relationship between the altitude of the sun and the hours of daylight. Finally, it was also they who developed the magnetic

variation and instrument. They produced even a cartographic grid on which both distance and direction to Makkah were correctly represented"

Abu Hanifah al-Dinawari (d. 282/895) compiled a comprehensive botanical lexicon known as *Kitab al-Nabat* (The Book of Plants), much before Greek works on the subject were translated into Arabic. It far surpasses the works of Greek scientists, such as Dioscorides and Theophrastus, on the subject. A German scholar Silverberg acknowledges the genius of al-Dinawari in the following words:

> "Anyhow it astonishes enough that the entire botanical literature of antiquity furnishes us only two parallels to our book (of Al-Dinawari). How was it that the Muslim people could, during so early a period of its literary life, attain the level of the people of such a genius as the Hellenic one, and even surpassed it in this respect"

INFLUENCE OF ISLAM ON WORLD CIVILISATION

The Arabs set an example of health care which is a crucial component of civilization. In this connection well-known German Orientalist Max Meyerhof wrote about the European hospitals of that time, comparing them with the conditions obtaining in Arab hospitals. Dr. Max says:

> "The Arab hospitals and the order existing in the Islamic countries of the past is giving us a lesson which is very unpleasant and leaves a bitter taste in our mouth. We cannot fully appreciate it unless we compare and contrast in minute details this system with that of the European hospitals of that period."

And he compares with it the conditions in one of the best hospitals of Europe, in Paris of the 18th century:

> "In one bed of moderate width, lay four, five or six persons besides each other, the feet of one to the head of other, children beside gray haired men; incredible but true, men and women intermingled together on the same couch, body against body, a woman groaned in the pangs of labour, a nursing infant writhed in convulsions, a typhus patient burnt in the delirium of fever, a consumptive (tuberculous) coughed hollowed cough and victim of some disease of skin tore with furious nails his infernally itching integument... The most miserable food was doled out to them in insufficient quantities and at irregular intervals...The building fairly swarmed with the most horrible vermin and the air of a morning was so vile in the sick wards that the attendants did not venture to enter them without a sponge saturated with vinegar held before their faces. The bodies of the dead ordinarily lay for 24 hours and often longer upon the death bed before they were removed."

SCIENTIFIC INSTITUTION

Scientific institutions, such as observatories, scientific academies, medical colleges, libraries and hospitals, which were established by Muslim rulers and members of the nobility and supported through *waqf* endowments, played a highly important role in the globalization of science. The most remarkable scientific institution in the early centuries of the Islamic era was *Bayt al-Hikmat* founded by Caliph Al-Mamun in Baghdad in the early decades of the 9th century. It was in this institution that nearly the whole corpus of scientific and philosophical literature from Greece, Persia and India was rendered into Arabic.

The translators of scientific and philosophical works included not only Muslims but also Jews, Christians, Sabaeans, Magians and Hindus. One of the most prolific translators was Hunayn ibn lshaq or Johannitus (d. 877), who was a Syrian Christian. 1t is significant to note that the seven volumes of Galen's *Anatomy* are available only in the form of its Arabic translation by Hunayn ibn Ishaq. Ibn Maymun or Maimonides (d. 1204), a brilliant scientist and translator, was a Spanish rabbi. Other important translators were Thabit ibn Qurra (d. 901), who was a Magian, Abu Bishr Matta (d. 940) and Qusta ibn Luqa (d. 912), both Christians, and Ali ibn Abbas Al-Majusi (d. 994), a Magian.

In his recent book *Identity and Violence: The Illusion of Destiny* (Penguin, 2006), the Indian Nobel Laureate Amartya Sen has paid handsome tributes to the role of Islamic civilization in the globalization of science and technology. To quote him:

"Muslim engineers were responsible for the development and use of the technology of irrigation in the form of *acequias* in Spain, drawing on the innovations they had introduced earlier in the dry lands in the Middle East. This allowed, more than a thousand years ago, the cultivation of crops, fruits and vegetables, and the pasturing of animals on what had earlier been completely dry European land. Indeed, Muslim technologists were in charge of this admirable technical job over many centuries.

Furthermore, Muslim mathematicians and scientists had a significant role in the globalization of technical knowledge through the movement of ideas across the Old World. For example, the decimal system and some early results in trigonometry went from India to Europe in the early years of the second millennium, transmitted through the works of Arab and Iranian mathematicians. Also, the Latin versions of the mathematical results of Indian mathematicians Aryabhata, Varahmihira and Brahmagupta, from their Sanskrit treatises produced between the fifth and seventh centuries appeared in Europe through two distinct steps, going first from Sanskrit to Arabic and then to Latin. Similarly, many of the Western classics, particularly from the ancient Greece, survived only through their Arabic translations, to be retranslated, mostly into Latin, in the early centuries of the second millennium, preceding the European Renaissance.

ISLAM'S MULTICULTURAL LEGACY IN SPAIN

The contribution of Islamic civilization to the promotion and advancement of knowledge, especially through an innovative amalgamation and creative synthesis of learning and science drawn from different sources, the creation of an environment of tolerance and accommodation, and to the onward march of human civilization-through the harvesting of nature's resources, science and medicine, engineering and technology, arts and crafts, architecture-constitutes one of the most illuminating chapters in human history. 1t is gratifying to note that there is now a growing recognition and appreciation of Islam's monumental role in the enrichment of human civilization.

Carly Fiorina, the then President of Hewlett Packard observed in a speech given on September 26, 2001:

> "When other nations were afraid of ideas, this civilization (of Islam) thrived on them, and kept them alive. When censors threatened to wipe out knowledge from past civilizations, this civilization kept the knowledge alive, and passed it on to others... . Although we are often unaware of our indebtedness to this civilization, its gifts are very much a part of our heritage. The technology industry would not exist without the contributions of the Arab mathematicians. Leaders like (the Ottoman Emperor) Sulayman the Magnificent contributed to our notions of tolerance and civic leadership. And perhaps we can learn a lesson from his example: it was leadership based on. meritocracy, not inheritance. It was leadership that harvested the full population that included Christian, Islamic and Jewish capabilities of very diverse traditions."

DUTY TOWARDS FUTURE

The glory of this great civilisation beckons its legatees to accept the challenge of contemporary situation and help humanity to break the shackles of misunderstanding, misinformation and misinterpretation of Islam. Why is the Muslim world unable to effectively counter the false notions prevailing within and around? We have to undertake an honest introspection. We seem to remain satisfied just by recalling our glorious past. It can help us regain self confidence but the solution of the problem lies in removing the deviations that have set in during the last seven centuries. It is true that the Mongol invasion destroyed the centres of Islamic civilization which led to the dispersal of leading Ulama and Sufis, the carriers of the message of the Prophet (PBUH). But have we done enough to overcome that loss?

The Prophet had warned—"God will not take away knowledge and learning all at once. Rather, he will take it away in such a way that, after the death of scholars, there will be no one left to fill up their place. People will then make the ignorant their leaders."

Is not the condition of Muslim masses the same today?

The result of this degeneration of so-called Islamic leadership is that two thirds of world's Muslim population is illiterate, far below the world average and even below that of the Third World. Three fourths of Muslim women are illiterate.

The reason obviously is that our Ulama lay more emphasis on the observation of rituals rather than instilling the substantial knowledge and meaning of the Qur'an and Hadith. The religious seminaries lay emphasis on memorising the word and ignore the meaning. Recently the Sachar Committee, set up by the Government of India, reported that the conditions of the Muslim masses are worse than Scheduled Castes and Scheduled Tribes. They have poor access to knowledge that can enable them to contribute to development and improve their living standard, what to speak of contribution to religious or natural sciences.

The proliferation of knowledge during the hey day of Islam owed to a large extent to the patronage of the rulers. Are the Muslim rulers today as solicitous of knowledge as those of yore. A pertinent example is the Nobel laureate Prof. Abdussalam. He was a brilliant student in undivided India and was lucky to get financial support from a fund created by a landlord Khizar Hayat Khan Tiwana. He had collected money to support the British war effort out of which a sum of fifteen lakhs remained unused when the war ended. Out of this

Abdussalam got Rs. 500.00 a month to pursue his education in Cambridge. It is noteworthy that after partition none of the Pakistanis got any help from this fund which shows the apathy of the rulers there. Nor has any of the landlords shown such imitative.

Government of India since independence has set up institutes of science and technology which have produced some leading nuclear scientists; the 12th President of our Republic Dr. Abdul Kalam is worthy example.

The world today is informed mostly by news agencies located in the West. According to an estimate, 80 per cent of news is supplied by these agencies. Do we have any agency that can put forward our view?

18

Islamic Law

The Ultimate Answer to Contemporary Questions

It's true that time is ever changing. In fact change itself is time. But it's also a fact that with all the ever-continuing change, time, in its essence, is beyond change. One can visualize it as a river where every wave is different from the other but still the river remains the same, which means that the river is the sum total of all the waves that represent change. But the absolute and permanent essence of Time is a metaphysical concept that is only for philosophers to contemplate. Human life, society and the common people, have to deal and come to terms with the change that may also be termed as the external expression of time.

Viewed in this context we come face to face with the spate of change that started taking place in the 19th century, gathered momentum in the 20th century and assumed revolutionary proportions during the later decades of the last century. Almost every sphere of human activity was affected by this change brought about by new scientific discoveries and inventions and technological advancement. The invention and development of the computer and computer technology and robots threw new challenges to human society. It was a challenge from the machine that man has himself invented and developed, and which was now behaving as if trying to break free from human control. Together with these developments were mind boggling advances in communication technology, medical science, biotechnology and space technology. All these changes were also challenges to human societies, cultures and traditions throughout the world.

The changes inspired by rapid advancement in science and technology were also challenges because they gave birth to rapid and enormous shifts in the ways human beings have so far been living, thinking, feeling and doing. The impact was almost ubiquitous, though its severity varied from place to place. Moreover these changes let loose the forces that tended to disturb the balance between the individual and society, between human ideals and actions and between the traditional scheme of things and ways to realize it. Among the societies and the people who largely believed in certain articles of faith and fashioned their life according to the guidance and values provided by this faith, Muslims and Muslim societies everywhere in the world were very prominent among the religious communities that found themselves at the receiving end of this deluge of change.

The problems caused by the change brought about by the revolutionary nature of science and technology were many and also far-reaching, and affected diverse fields of thought and action—social, cultural, moral, economic, and political, in Muslim societies the world over. Some problems were unprecedented like those posed by the new advances in medical science, bio-sciences and genetics like cloning. The successful cloning of animals led to the claims of human cloning which involves a lot of ethical, social and religio-legal questions. Likewise, there was the issue of insurance that gradually took various forms as life, business, property, health, and education insurance, etc. All this involved general trade practices as well as some forms of betting but at the same time had many aspects of cooperation and help. Thus, insurance also needed a clear decree from Islamic point of view. At the political front, more and more Muslims living in plural societies where non-Muslims are dominant posed the questions of Muslim participation in governance in non-Muslim dominated states.

Besides new and unprecedented situations and questions, new complications have developed within the traditional and well established practices. Participation of Muslims in various social activities involving non-Muslims, co-education and mixing of sexes in places of work, misuse of *talaq* in the Muslim society, problem of missing husbands, situations in trade and commerce where interest cannot be avoided, violation of various Islamic laws in business deals finalized through telephone and internet, non-Islamic trade practices, many new medical and surgical advances like organ transplant, cloning, sperm and ova banking, artificial pregnancy and birth, AIDS and related issues, mercy killing, etc. are only some of the ever growing number of questions that make living a Islamic life in the present world problematic.

Another area where external changes impacted the most was the problems faced by the Muslims living under non-Muslim domination. All Muslim minorities faced almost similar questions and crises and this situation called for devising a new intellectual and Islamic response. This demand resulted in the development of what is termed as 'Minority Fiqh' which is still in its infancy but needs to be develooped into a full-fledged jurisprudential discipline.

Away from these exclusively Muslim issues, there are also the predicaments and dilemmas that are shared by the entire mankind. The changes brought about by the forces unleashed by the industrial revolution resulted in the devaluation of human dignity. The rapid urbanization gave birth to crowds in which human beings were drowned with all the grace and worth of their thought and action. In big cities everybody was now an individual. This growth of individualism resulted in the breakdown of the family system which in turn devastated the entire web of human relations and disturbed the social equilibrium. On the economic front, the rise of capitalism saw the wealth being concentrated in a few hands while the masses of people became poorer day by day. In politics, totalitarian states usurped human freedom in the name of collective welfare while the democracies turned into monocracies. The emergence of mass media resulted in loosening of public morals and sexual license.

It is not that no efforts were made to grapple with these questions and come out with possible solutions. Both the religious and secular quarters came forward with multiple ways of correcting the situation. Some betterment does seem to have been brought about here and there but the overall situation is still quite depressing. The main reason for these ameliorative efforts not bearing the desired fruits is that all these approaches touch only the surface and refuse to penetrate the depth of the problem.

This brings us to the Islamic approach that, view objectively, proves to be comprehensive and holistic as it does not touch the problem merely from outside but delves deep into its causes. Moreover, while attempting a solution it gives primacy to the objectives and impacts of the effort. What distinguishes the Islamic approach from other approaches and makes it more rewarding is its emphasis on accountability and awakening of conscience. The concept of being answerable to the divine authority makes a man be good and righteous even if one is away from the long arm of the laws of the world. The Islamic approach strikes at the very roots of the problem and brings forth a solution that satisfies all the demands of justice.

The Islamic approach is based on the divine principles enshrined in the Qur'an and Sunnah. These principles provide general guidance and framework, adherence to which is essential. Because of being general and directive in nature, these principles, have a lot of flexibility. That's why they are able to provide answers to questions posed at any time or place.

Islamic guidance and sanctions are compositely called the Islamic Law. Islamic Law is based on the *mohkam* (absolute) verses of the Qur'an and authenticated hadiths. This Law encompasses all aspects and affairs of life. It provides both the mandatory and prohibitory sanctions for a better management of the human society. Islamic Law fulfills five broad objectives that aim at the overall welfare of mankind. These objectives concern protecting and safeguarding life, property, religion, intellectual achievements and welfare of the entire mankind. In religious terms, these objectives are called the Objectives of Shariah.

There has been a strong and brilliant tradition of law making in light of these objectives, nurtured and consolidated by experts of Islamic law and great interpreters of Islam. With all the purity of heart and strength of mind, they applied themselves to their utmost not only to derive solutions of the contemporary issues but also laid down a methodology to serve as a guidance for successive generations. As there was complete freedom of thought and expression in the early Islamic society and expert scholars were free to exert their creative powers to interpret Islamic principles according to the exigencies of the time, there came into being different approaches of interpretation and law making. These approaches were later institutionalized into schools of jurisprudence. Although these schools differ from one another in matters of understanding and interpreting the two fundamental sources of Islam - Qur'an and Hadith, even go contradicting each other at certain places, but they agree on one point — the Objectives of Shariah, as it is the only source that they draw their sanction and justification from. These objectives were so sacrosanct and dear to them that they changed their course of interpretation if they saw it violating these objectives. It was to avoid such situations arising out of *Qiyas* (analogical reasoning) that the great Islamic jurist Imam Abu Hanifa devised the method of *Istihsan* which became the basis for deriving religio-legal rulings in many cases. The Maliki and Hanbali schools also apply the principle of *Istihsan*, though with certain qualifications. Many scholars agree that the Shafi'i School too recognizes it. The creative juristic device — the principle of *Istislah,* is yet another method of being faithful to the Objectives of Shariah, the Maliki school being more known for applying it.

Shah Waliullah (1703-1755) is one of the greatest mujaddids

(renewer) and mujtahids of Islam in the Indian sub-continent who has many firsts in the field of religious revival to his credit. One of his many path breaking contributions to the renewal of Islamic thought was his stupendous effort to bring different schools of Islamic jurisprudence closer to each other, by presenting his own juristic approach that eclectically benefited from all the schools. He was gifted with a foresight that could go beyond his own times to know that the coming centuries would face a spate of problems which may not be tackled exclusively by any one school of jurisprudence. He knew fully well that every school had certain positions and devices that could be of use where other schools did not offer any guidance which means that if all the schools are made to share a common platform they would together be able to provide answers to all questions that are brought for their consideration. Shah Waliullah has attempted this synthesis in his pioneering works like *Hujjatullahil Baligha, Fuyuzul Harmain, Al-Tafhimatul Ilahiya,* Al-Insaf fi *Bayan* Sabab-al Ikhtilaf where he has tried to bring compatibility between fiqh and hadith and between juristic efforts and hadith.

This pioneering creative initiative of Shah Waliullah not only helped later Islamic jurists engaged in finding solutions to new problems but also gave them confidence to attempt such a challenging innovation by providing them with a paradigm to fall back upon as a supporting authority. In fact the Waliullahi paradigm is serving as a guiding star for the individuals and institutions wedded to the task of attempting ijtihad for providing Islamic solutions. Premier world Islamic juristic bodies such as, Majmual Fiqh Aalamal Islami ad Daula, Jeddah, Fiqh Academy of the Rabta Aalamal Islami, Ifta Council, Europe and Islamic Fiqh Academy, India are working with the Waliullah methodology as a basis. These organizations have already proved the efficacy of this method by offering satisfactory Islamic answers to many vexing questions facing Muslims the world over. The solutions to questions about insurance, particularly medical insurance offered by the Ifta

Council, Europe, International Fiqh Academy, Jeddah's solutions to many questions posed by the new medical devices and solutions about questions regarding powers of the *wali* (guardian) in nikah, forced marriage, pronouncing *talaq* in the state of intoxication etc. offered by the Islamic Fiqh Academy, India are only a few outstanding examples of the success of this eclectic approach exemplified by Shah Waliullah.

Problems faced by the Muslim minorities all over the world are one area where application of this methodology can be most rewarding since these problems are related to diverse nationalities, politics and milieus, they demand a highly multi-layered response and a multi-pronged approach. Muslim-non-Muslim relations are a very important component of the Muslim minority discourse and here also this synergizing approach may be put to tremendous uses.

But to be able to attempt this more challenging task the Muslims must first try to set their own house in order by smoothening the rough ends of the various schools of jurisprudence and effecting a happy coming together among them. This alone can present to the world the Islamic fiqh and Islamic juristic genius as one unified and composite intellectual whole, capable of continuously renewing the Islamic creed and practice to keep them relevant for all times and places. In view of the civilizational and intellectual crises that the world is facing today, there is no doubt that it is only Islam that can provide lasting and satisfactory solutions. But for this to happen and be a fact of life, Muslims themselves will have to shed their intellectual lethargy and revive their creative genius.

Index